THE HOUSES OF KEY WEST

THE HOUSES OF KEY WEST

ALEX CAEMMERER

PINEAPPLE PRESS
SARASOTA, FLORIDA

TO LI, JOHN, ALEX, AND BILL

Inquiries should be addressed to:
Pineapple Press, Inc.
P.O. Box 3889
Sarasota, FL 34230
www.pineapplepress.com

Library of Congress Cataloging-in-Publication Data

Caemmerer, Alex, 1923-
    Houses of Key West / Alex Caemmerer—1st ed.
      p. cm.
      Includes bibliographical references (p.   ).
      ISBN 1-56164-009-3 : $18.95
1. Architecture.Domestic—Florida—Key West. 2.Archi-
tecture, Modern—19th century—Florida—Key West.
3. Vernacular architecture—Florida—Key West.
4. Key West (Fla.)—Buildings, structures, etc. I.
Title.
NA7238.N48C34
728'.37'0975941—dc20

                                        91-42369
                                        CIP

First Edition   10 9 8 7 6

Design by Wendy McMillan
Printed in China

CONTENTS

Acknowledgments

In showing recognition of my source material and thanking those who have helped me in this project, I would first like to thank the Florida Keys Historic Preservation Board of Trustees for their permission to use material from their Cultural Resource Survey of Key West, upon which I relied heavily. It is a comprehensive study of the "built environment" of Key West.

I would also like to thank Dr. William Carl Shiver, architectural consultant on the Cultural Resource Survey Team, now historic sites specialist with the Florida Bureau of Historic Preservation, for his valuable assistance in identifying the architectural styles and details of the houses presented in this book. I also wish to thank Tom Hambright, Director of Local and State History of the Monroe County Library at Key West for his help in researching this book. And many thanks to Ronald Haase, professor of architectural history at the University of Florida, for reading the manuscript and providing helpful improvements.

And then there are those individuals who provided much anecdotal material about specific houses. Key West is a city of old families, some of whom have occupied their houses for generations. Some members of the present generation are descendants of the original settlers and have generously passed on to me stories handed down to them from previous generations. I want to thank the following: Gary Blum, Betty Bruce, Philip Burton, Ed Cox, Francis Delaney, Shirley Freeman, Jerry Goodman, Richard Motley, Carol O'Connell, Jeane Porter, Lucien Proby, Charles Ramos, Ramona Santiago, and Mary Spottswood.

I would also like to thank my editor, June Cussen, for her patience as well as editorial expertise in producing this book with me.

FOREWORD

The architecture of Key West and the charm of this faraway island retreat have been beguiling to each of us lucky enough to have spent some time there. For Alex Caemmerer it has been so compelling a place that he has returned again and again to walk its narrow streets and drink deeply of its architectural riches. Not content to simply watch and wonder, Dr. Caemmerer has spent long hours in the Key West library and in the Avery Library at Columbia University digging into the history of styles, precedents, and personalities that brought such a dense consistency to the architecture of this jewel in the chain of rocks called the Florida Keys. He shares with us the labors of his research in this beautiful volume.

As you read and enjoy this book you will be reminded of how complex and tangled was the architecture of the 19th century. The kaleidoscope of eclectic styles which came from this era ranged from the formality of Greek Revival to the picturesque composition of Victorian sensibilities. The visual leitmotif which ties such extremes together is the austere wood-frame vernacular of no-nonsense homes built by ship's carpenters, some prefabricated and carried long distances over sea, which have never known the sweep of a paint brush across their raw cypress siding.

Dr. Caemmerer untangles this yarn of history for us and lays out a logical architectural lineage that helps the visitor or the resident of Key West to better understand the character of this beautiful place. We are all indebted to him for his effort. As such, this book should be required reading placed on every nightstand or in every backpack on the island.

Ronald W. Haase
Professor of Architecture
University of Florida

PREFACE

My first contact with Key West came in the mid-fifties after a long drive from New York City down the Atlantic coast to the 160-mile-long Overseas Highway, then a two-lane, asphalt road connecting a string of barren islands by a series of rickety bridges. At one spot the road ran on top of an old railroad trestle bridge, one of the last remnants of the Flagler Overseas Railway. I had been called up in the doctors' draft during the Korean Crisis and ordered to report to the U.S. Naval Hospital at Key West for a two-year tour of duty. Almost everything in Key West at the time was referred to as Southernmost, and it wasn't long before I was referred to as the "Southernmost Psychiatrist."

The city in those days was over-run by some 20,000 servicemen, mostly naval personnel and their dependents. Duval street was a mass of white sailor's uniforms, with the ubiquitous MPs strolling up and down monitoring the numerous bars, the center of the sailors' social life in town. Otherwise, Key West was a sleepy tropical island, best described then, as now, as "laid back." Key West was known as a remote place where artists and writers could find quiet, isolation, and escape from the conventions of the rest of the country. Tennessee Williams, for example, was one of Key West's most famous citizens. While I was there they were filming Williams's *Rose Tattoo* with Anna Magnani and Burt Lancaster, and we all watched the proceedings with great interest, as there weren't many other diversions at that time in Key West.

The town consisted of essentially two areas: the "old town," that square mile or so of the southwestern part of the island, bounded by Truman Avenue and White Street, which later came to be designated officially as the historic section; and the newer area, on the Atlantic side, extending east to the bridge connecting the island to the north. Modern housing in Key West was easily distinguished from the old. New construction was mostly concrete block with stucco and usually ranch-style, a practical type of housing in a tropical climate with ubiquitous termite infestation. This area was occupied mostly by either naval families or permanent residents, the former housed mostly in multiple-family naval housing complexes, and the latter in one-story, one-family, stuccoed concrete-block houses surrounded by lawns and palm trees—looking like suburban Florida.

Old Town consisted of a concentration of nineteenth-century houses in various states of disrepair, largely due to the ravages of the tropical weather combined with the prohibitive cost of maintenance so essential in the tropics, a particular burden in a community which had suffered from recurrent economic down-swings over the years. The local economy depended mostly on the naval presence, with some income from fishing, shrimping, and what little tourism accompanied the winter season. Key West was not yet popular as a place for second or retirement homes. The beauties of the island—its climate, atmosphere, isolation, exotic flora, and finally, its unique architecture—had not yet caught on with the travelling public, and therefore the economic means of adequately protecting, maintaining, and refurbishing the lovely old homes was not what it is today.

Naval personnel had little contact with the locals, as servicemen had their own quarters, eating places, commissary, amusements and sports, etc. We didn't get to spend much time in the old section of town. However, one could not miss seeing the incredible collection of old wooden houses jammed together on the city streets and I was increasingly attracted to and struck by their beautiful design. Especially intriguing were the eyebrow houses, with their front porch roofs extending demurely over the second-story windows, hence the term eyebrow. I have discovered that they are unique to Key West and are not found anywhere else in the country.

What particularly impressed me at the time was that, although many of these houses were small and owned by people of modest means—mostly local workers, they had a simplicity of line and an aura of elegance and dignity which had the same effect on one as does, for instance, a simple Bach tune. The classic proportions and lines of these old Key West houses, especially the eyebrow houses, so intrigued me back then, that I knew someday I would want to come back to this place.

Many years, a wife and three sons later, I found myself driving the 160 miles of Overseas Highway again to visit Key West one February in the late sixties for a winter vacation. By that time, although Key West had changed,

changed considerably, it had not been entirely for the better. The two-mile strip of what was once salt flats stretching from the bridge to Old Town was now a series of malls, auto dealerships, motels, and other modern commercial establishments looking much like any other highway strip on the mainland. The commercial center of town had left Duval Street and moved north to the highway malls. Duval Street was all but deserted, with litter blowing down the street and not much else going on. The Navy had virtually abandoned the area in the late 1950s, taking with it the financial support on which the local economy depended. Consequently, the residential areas, especially Old Town, showed further evidence of deterioration. The beautiful old houses were showing their age—paint was not very much in evidence, and many looked abandoned. We didn't know it then, but it was at about that time that serious measures were being adopted to preserve and restore old Key West to a collection of some of the most impressive architectural specimens to be found anywhere in the country.

Skipping some years, I found myself again returning to Key West in the late seventies. By that time considerable changes had taken place in Key West. The climate was still lovely, the restaurants even better, and there were increasing signs that Key West was on an upswing. Duval Street had been revitalized and now looked like a downtown shopping mall—in some areas it was quite upscale. A large number of the old houses in the historic area had been tastefully restored, and many others were in the process. The area was already being traversed regularly by the ubiquitous conch trains, those descendants of the old world's fair trains, taking tourists through the streets of the island with a guide pointing out all the sights of interest—especially the old houses.

We have been returning to Key West ever since, each year following the progress of the restoration of the old houses. Fortuitously, a few years ago, my wife gave me an automatic camera of the "point-and-push" type. I began photographing some of the more interesting and esthetically appealing houses in the area. Those first shots resulted in the publication of a series of Key West postcards. I acquired a much more serious Canon 650EOS Single Lens Reflex camera, which allows for better com-position work and wide-angle shots, and continued with notecards and a poster. The next project seemed like a natural—a book-length collection of photographs of the most photogenic and historically important of the old houses of Key West—and here it is. It has taken a great deal of effort in research and writing in addition to photography, but it has been very exciting. I hope my readers will enjoy it as much as I have enjoyed doing it.

INTRODUCTION

Key West, Florida, is a small city of some 25,000 people located on the last of a chain of coral islands, the Florida Keys, stretching about 160 miles southwest of Miami into the Gulf of Mexico. It is closer to Cuba than to the mainland of the United States. Measuring about 2 miles by 4 miles, Key West is the most prominent and populous, oldest established, and interesting of the islands and serves as the county seat of Monroe County—the county of the Keys. Governed by a mayor and council, it is pretty much a self-contained city, with comprehensive public services and a broad variety of commercial establishments, recreational facilities, cultural resources, and a highly developed and richly supported tourist base.

The last two decades in particular have seen many changes in Key West. There has been a concerted effort to restore and preserve the officially designated historic section of the city, which in turn has contributed significantly to an ever-growing tourist interest. This has resulted in many more hotel and motel facilities on the island, and a considerable building boom to satisfy the increasing demand for second as well as retirement homes. During these years, many of the nineteenth-century homes in the historic section were carefully restored to their original condition. The process has gradually transformed the previously dilapidated area to a veritable architectural museum. Controls were put in place early enough to see to it that all construction in the historic district preserved its original appearance and character. The area has now become one of the most popular tourist attractions on the island.

As this process continued, the other changes in Key West naturally followed, transforming Key West from a quiet and easy-going tropical island to a bustling, cosmopolitan resort city. However, it still maintains its "laid-back" character and charm, due at least in part to the unusual and distinctive architecture of Old Town. But, of course, its nearly ideal winter climate will always be its greatest attraction.

As for the people of Key West, there is diversity in almost every category—age, life-style, ethnic origin, occupation, as well as social and economic status. It is a place of individuals and almost agressive individuality, and one is never surprised with the new and different as it emerges ineluctably in Key West. Most of what appears is both accepted and enjoyed. Everyone seems to get along in spite of such differences. There is no dress code—you can wear just about anything, anywhere, at any time. Naturally, all this makes for a very heterogeneous population, the extreme fringes of which can verge into the quaint, the bizarre, and, unfortunately, sometimes the unruly. Of further interest is the fact that visitors from Europe and Asia are now visiting Key West in large numbers, adding an international flavor.

In spite of it all, there pervades in Key West a certain small-town atmosphere of friendliness and mutual interest in keeping it like it is. One can enjoy just walking the sidewalks, assured of coming upon new and engaging sights. There are little alleyways that reveal all sorts of unusual and interesting buildings—tiny gerry-built shacks, cottages of every description, and other remnants of the old cigar-maker days. What strikes one most is that no matter what the size, shape, location, or state of disrepair, most of the buildings have interesting form and design. Around the corner may sit an arrestingly beautiful classic architectural specimen—which was probably designed and built by a local carpenter with an exceptionally good eye. A walk though Old Town is never dull to the appreciative connoisseur of things that look good and are well made. There is something fundamental about the simple designs of these houses which transcends the more materialistic architectural aspects of size, grandeur, or opulence.

This book offers a selection of what are probably the most historically interesting, esthetically appealing, and photogenic of the nineteenth-century houses in the Key West historic district. There are literally hundreds of individual houses in the district, too numerous to portray in their entirety. Some are examples of well-known architectural styles, whereas others were completely individually conceived, either by design or chance—mostly the latter, it seems.

I have attempted to provide some text on the methods of construction and the architectural styles of these Key West houses. Since I am not an architectural historian, I must leave the definitive study of this important topic to those who are (and this is a book that deserves to be written). But my hope is that what is written here will in the meantime fill a gap and offer a pictorial study of the wonderfully fascinating houses of Key West.

THE HOUSES OF KEY WEST

RESTORATION

The fact that there now exists in Key West a large collection of nineteenth-century houses which have been faithfully and beautifully restored is by no means due to mere chance. Much of the rebuilding and restoring of these old houses has occurred in the past twenty-five years, subject to strict regulation by the various federal, state, and local governmental agencies which have been created to see to it that the architecture of the historic area is preserved and restored as close to its original state as possible. There has been a general movement in this direction throughout the country, with the creation of many historic districts under the protection of regulatory agencies mandated to preserve their historic authenticity.

614 Fleming Street

Right: Eyebrow house, unrestored. This rather large five-bay Classical Revival eyebrow house has been in the Haskins family since it was built in the 1880s. It has recently changed hands and has enjoyed a complete and elegant restoration.

614 Fleming Street

Left: Eyebrow house, restored

524 Frances Street
The House of Seven Gables

Above: This Victorian-Gothic Revival house was built for himself in 1907 by the carpenter-architect Kennedy, who designed the enormous, high-style Curry mansion on Eaton Street. After his death it was occupied for many years by his daughter, Ida Kennedy. It came into less-than-caring hands for a while and had deteriorated badly until it was acquired in the 1980s by the present owners and occupants, Lynn and David Kaufelt. Along with contractors Cheryl Troxel and Jeff Nablo, the Kaufelts did an extensive job of restoring and remodelling to combine old-time Key West with contemporary feel and convenience. The original plan of the house was unaltered: Victorian, with its turned balustrades, dentil mouldings, etc., but the high-pitched gable roofline is more Gothic Revival in character.

As early as the 1930s, when Key West was in the midst of its worst economic decline, Key Westers realized that they had an architectural treasure trove in their midst and were granted funds from the Federal Relief Administration to help restore Key West's "indigenous architecture, historic background, and intangible charm," to quote the grantor's words. This was meant to revive the economy of the island by making it more attractive to tourists. But these early attempts were not very far-reaching for the domestic architecture of the area.

Many years passed before more formal and specific action was taken. World War II came and brought with it a great expansion of the military establishment in Key West, and along with it, a real shot in the arm to the economy. Much new contemporary building was done and with the re-employment of much of the work force, maintenance of the historic house inventory at least kept abreast of the ravages of time and weather. After the war came another decline, to be followed by yet another temporary upswing during the Korean episode. However, the Navy essentially left the area again in the late 1950s, withdrawing an important source of economic strength from Key West.

It was during the forties that some organized efforts came into play which eventually have led to the remarkable renaissance in the historic area of Key West. In 1948, the Key West Art and Historical Society was formed. They managed to preserve the two Martello Towers built in 1861 at the northeastern end of the island. The East Tower still houses the museum of the Art and Historical Society.

In 1959 the beautiful and impressive Caroline Lowe House was destroyed by fire and the old Geiger house was about to be replaced by a service station. The latter had been used by John James Audubon during his visit to Key West in the 1830s. These two events served to arouse the interested citizenry of Key West, and the Old Island Restoration Foundation was founded to attract interest in saving the historic homes in town as well as exploit them as a tourist attraction.

In 1965 the City Commission established the Old Island Restoration Commission. It was charged with the responsibility for the preservation of historic buildings in the old section of Key West. Its powers included architectural review over any new construction or alterations to structures within the old section.

In 1966 Congress passed the National Historic Preservation Act that created a National Register of districts, sites, buildings, and such, designated as historic. In Florida, the Division of Archives, History and Records Management administers the National Register program. In 1972, the Florida Legislature created another state agency, the Historic Key West Preservation Board of Trustees (now the Florida Keys Preservation Board of Trustees) to deal specifically with Key West. For some time this authority was not used, as the Old Island Restoration Commission was still functioning at that time. However, since 1986 these duties have been taken over by the present Historic Architectural Review Commission which continues to keep a tight rein on all projects planned in the historic areas of Key West.

One can see that a gradually increasing interest has been shown in the architecture of Key West, first by concerned citizens, and then by the city, state, and finally, the federal government, all of have by this time have become appropriately impressed by Key West's historic heritage and have made comprehensive and concerted efforts and taken appropriate steps to see to it that it is preserved for all to enjoy.

The actual building and restoration of the houses was, of course, done or paid for by individuals who invested their time and money in the local real estate. The effort snowballed, for as the early restoration projects were accomplished, more and more investors were attracted to the area and more and more restoration projects were started. Real estate values have steadily increased over the years, helped along by the appearance of more and more exquisitely restored properties. The process feeds on itself and the collection of authentic restorations continues to grow. One cannot walk very far in Key West without seeing a major building project under way, either an addition or a cosmetic restoration. Along with these projects has come completely new construction in various areas, much of which is designed to fit in with the architecture of the older homes. Every project in the historic district must be approved by the Historic Architectural Review Commission, which maintains strict guidelines and controls over every aspect of building in the historic area. Detailed plans must be presented which are carefully evaluated and must meet detailed specifications. All this has paid off, as the historic district of Key West is now one of its most famous and valuable attractions.

Left: 628 Frances Street
Right: 804 Caroline Street

628 Frances Street is an excellent prototype of the temple-form Classical Revival with the incised portico and pediment and is probably similar to many early Key West houses as suggested by John Whitehead's drawings of 1838. There are many houses like this one in Key West today. Most date from after the fire of 1886 and are probably duplicates of those which burned down. This plan was popular for multiple usage with commercial space on the first floor and living quarters on the second. 804 Caroline Street (The Jefferson Adams House) could look like 628 Frances after a restoration, except for the detailing. This is one of the few remaining truly Classical Revival houses in the official historic district in such a neglected state.

CONSTRUCTION

A discussion of house construction in the historic section of Key West must include something about its architecture, since much, if not most, of the planning and building was done without the help of professional architects. The builders were their own architects as well as carpenters and contractors. Many of the early Key West houses were either copies of a previous building or modifications of other buildings in town. Since most of Key West's early houses were locally conceived and executed according to local tastes and fashions, they are largely and best described as vernacular architecture. Typical Key West houses are also referred to as Conch houses, the generic term for anything native to the island.

A few generalizations can be made in regard to the basic design and construction of the early Key West houses that seem to set them apart from domestic architecture of the rest of the country. Key West seems to be different from the rest of the country in a lot of ways, when you come to think of it. One would expect that, in a community with the obvious wealth of Key West, there would be at least a few rather spectacular and impressive homes, perhaps even designed by well-known architects. Certainly, there would be quite a number of large dwellings such as one usually finds in cities the size of Key West. However, Key West has no homes of such distinction or architectural pre-eminence to even compare with examples seen in other parts of the country.

On the other hand, it would be hard to find in any small city such a large collection of small, and even very small, homes with such elegance of design, character, dignity, and beauty of line, as on this small island. Key West was really an industrial town and most of its inhabitants were workers who had little to spend on housing. Everywhere else it seems to be generally true that smaller houses are less impressive esthetically—mostly because economizing is the most important consideration in their construction. Good design is expensive. Most houses are built without the aid of expert architectural services, and many are merely slightly modified copies or clones of a rather mundane design to start with. As with most manufactured items, inexpensive products do not get the services of good designers. However, in Key West, this is not so. The reason lies in Key West's history.

The builders of the individual houses in old Key West were usually ships' carpenters who were called upon to build homes for their captains who settled in Key West. As Starr points out in his article, "The Carpenter-Architects of Key West":

> Key West's domestic buildings are essentially American in still another sense: No professional architect designed them— no one, in fact designed them at all. They are a spectacular result of carpenter architecture, made by men without formal training who had studied no abstract tables of the strength of the materials and who probably solved the details of design as they built. Their design tables were in their thumbs, their schooling consisted of memories of other buildings, seen in other places, that had accomplished what the carpenters needed. Because they worked in Key West, the carpenter-architects brought with them memories of a number of vessels and seaport homes from their own past. They borrowed from what they wanted: widow's walks from New England; roof scuttles for ventilation from ships themselves; long, overhanging eaves ands gutters connected to underground cisterns from the West Indies. From these, and from the echoes of fashion that made their way to Key West with its new arrivals over 150 years of history, they derived from time to time a suggestion of contemporary styles: Greek Revival columns and Federal fanlights; later, from the Gothic Revival, gables and window bays; from Creole New Orleans, wrought-iron trellises and balustrades, reproducing these, with tropical fecundity of imagination, in wood.

The present collection of nineteenth-century homes are of frame construction and, for the most part, were built between 1886 and 1912. In 1886 there was a huge fire that destroyed more than half of the buildings in Key West. Not much is known about those structures built before the Great Fire of 1886 except most likely they were very similar to the structures that replaced them. Early drawings indicate that they were mostly Classical Revival structures of the temple design. Of particular interest is the fact that, although so much if it was destroyed in the fire, the town was rebuilt in wood, rather than more fire-resistant materials. Dade County pine was perhaps the most desirable and widely used wood in the better homes, as the high resin content made it almost impervious to the ubiquitous flying termites of Key West. It was even used rather than plaster for walls and ceilings. This is not the usual pattern in other cities that have experienced such a fire. However, as Starr writes:

> Wood, of course, constitutes the essential material of the carpenter-architect. Wood was available in Key West, even though little structural-sized timber grows locally. Some came to the city from the salvage of wrecks, the city's first major doomed industry. Some of these wrecks had been carrying structural-grade lumber from Pensacola and its nearby forests. The cargoes were usually auctioned off in Key West, in part to pay the salvage bill. Lumber was also deliberately imported by Key Westers with the money they made in other transactions—mahogany from Honduras, cypress from the upper Keys near the Florida mainland; pine from the Gulf coast ports like Pensacola, Mobile, and Pasagoula.

There is an even more obvious answer to why Key Westers rebuilt using wood, and that is that there were no local governmental agencies in place at that time. Each rebuilder made his own decision based generally on economy and convenience. As there was little or no insurance coverage on most of the burned buildings, strict economizing was required.

The surviving nineteenth-century houses seem to fall into only a few architectural styles, many resembling each other both inside and out. They have either one, one and a half, or two stories and attic—rarely three stories. They present a street-side facade with at least some decorative ele-

418 William Street

Right: This four-bay vernacular variation on a Classical Revival theme resembles a Creole cottage because of the double entrances on the incised porch on the long street facade. It is a common arrangement in New Orleans folk houses. Its only decorations are the plain capitals on the porch supports. Even the balusters are plain. It appears to be a carpenter-designed one-of-a-kind Key Wester of unclear derivation. It epitomizes the snugness of a ship's carpenter influence. Note the hatches on the roof.

ments but have few architectural details of interest on the other three sides. Not much individual imagination is in evidence, and no great variations are present except, perhaps, in the balustrades or gingerbread decorations. Few personal elements of design, shape, or embellishment are seen. Yet the houses are beautiful, especially if one sees them collectively. Perhaps this was by accident, and perhaps not.

Most Key West houses have a rectangular floor plan which, for the most part, are of two basic designs: the central hall and the side hall. As we have noted, ships' captains from New England, the Carolinas, and the Bahamas often had their ships' carpenters build their

houses—which may well account for the almost uniformly symmetrical designs. In the writer's opinion, it is the symmetry that is probably the most important factor contributing to the beauty of Key West Houses. After all, most of the elegant and impressive New England colonials, as well as many of the Greek Revivals, are essentially symmetrical. Symmetry gives balance and projects strength.

Metal nails were scarce in those days; houses were put together by mortise and tenon joints and wooden pegs, techniques known in furniture-making as joinery. Houses of this construction are better able to withstand storms and hurricanes than buildings put together with metal nails. The latter allow for little give in a high wind. Key West houses resemble furniture in certain other ways: they are snug, trim, and show economy of design, shape, and material—much like ships, also. Inasmuch as many houses, for example the eyebrow houses, resemble each other, one might guess that the same contractors built a number of them, duplicating their work much as modern day developers do. We know that the Roberts family had several eyebrows built in town at about the same time.

Another factor which influenced house-building was the availaby of land. The building lots in town were usually very narrow, and most houses were built leaving little or no side yards. There were no building codes to restrict land use, so many houses were of the townhouse type—deep, with very small side-yard clearance. After all, there was no need for a driveway in those days. This is now somewhat of a disadvantage, as there is almost no off-street parking in Key West. It is also said that in the nineteenth century some Key Westers were still afraid of unfriendly Indians, so they would rather have the protection of a close neighbor than an expanse of lawn. Of course, other considerations must have been on their minds, such as distance from the center of town. Larger lots were too far out. Since many of the most popular houses were built for workers on small tracts of land by owners of the cigar factories, luxurious accommodations they were not. There is very high density in the cigar-makers' tracts, often with narrow lanes dividing blocks in the middle in order to use every square foot of space for building sites.

Another phenomenon of note is the nearness of most houses to the street. This may be due to the fact that most Key West houses had other buildings on the property—separate buildings for the kitchen and outhouse. In many instances there had been an earlier, smaller building on the property which was either replaced with a more elaborate and larger house or added to later on. The older buildings were often moved to the rear of the lot to serve as an addition to the newer building, incorporated into the plan as a kitchen, for instance. We also know that some houses were built along dirt paths planned for streets before their eventual width was known. Wherever there is a substantial setback, the house has probably been moved, as with the enormous Curry-Freeman house—the only one on the block that has a generous front yard. Many houses in Key West were originally one story and have been increased to two or two and a half. There are very few houses over three stories in town.

The most ubiquitous architectural phenomenon in Key West houses is the presence of porches. Almost all have a porch, usually extending the entire width of the street facade. In the case of two-story houses, there is usually also a gallery—that is, a porch under the main roof of the house on the second story. Many have two-story porches on two or even three sides. Where a porch extends to another facade, it is called a veranda. The desirability of porches is easily understood in a tropical climate. The porch not only keeps the house cooler, but provides additional outside living space in warm weather as well as offering more opportunities for socializing with passersby. The latter is also reputed to be a reason for building houses close to the street.

The island of Key West is composed of solid limestone, the only natural rock around. Excavation is difficult, and there are almost no excavated basements in town. Cisterns are usually only half below ground level. In fact, utilities in Key West are above ground for this reason. Buildings have to be firmly anchored however, and in Key West most rest on quarried solid limestone blocks (piers), usually measuring 10 inches by 10 inches and 18 inches high, to which they are pinned. These piers rest on the ground, stabilized by the solid limestone under the thin layer of Key West's topsoil. Some piers are made of wood or brick. Houses are thus raised above ground, to allow for the high winds of storms and hurricanes to pass under as well as to keep the house out of flood waters. It is now required on many of the keys that new construction be a full story above high water mark. Usually the area below the house is covered with lattice work or pickets.

Except for a few of the larger houses, there are almost no chimneys in Key West. Fireplaces are not needed in the year-round warm climate. The chimneys in Key West were mostly in outside kitchen buildings, put there for two obvious reasons—to keep the heat of the kitchen away from the house and as a fire-preventive measure.

The two types of local frame construction are "braced frame" and "balloon frame" construction. The braced frame consists of heavy vertical corner posts framed into the sills and rising to support the roof plate. Horizontal girders are framed into the corner posts at each story to support the floor load. All of these members are joined together by mortise and tenon joints, making for a strong, rigid, box frame. The entire frame rests directly on the corner foundation piers.

In balloon frame construction multiple vertical studs are fastened by machine-made nails to the sills and carry the weight of the roof plate. Floor joists rest on the roof plate, supported by the studs. This is is the most common modern frame construction in the rest of the United States. (However, modern construction in Key West is more apt to be concrete block with stucco, rather than frame.)

Exterior siding is usually horizontal clapboard or over-lapping weather-board. Occasionally one sees vertical board-and-batten sheathing in Victorian-style houses, and often a variety of exterior sheathing from one part of a house to another. Also, although the facade of a house may have conventional siding, the other sides may vary according to what was available or economical at the time.

Plaster was not used for interior walls, as it was found that the shifting of the house caused by heavy storm winds caused cracking, so that wood sheathing, square-edged or tongued and grooved, either horizontal or vertical, was used. (In the 1920s this kind of wall was considered out of style, so the beautiful grained wood was often covered over with beaver-board and then painted.)

Most windows in Key West are double-hung, six-light windows similar to those in New England Colonial houses. Blinds with movable louvers are common, to allow for cooling breezes to pass through.

The typical peaked or hip-roof of Key West houses helps in cooling by providing a layer of air insulation in the attic. Gable openings and scuttles, hatchlike openings in the roof, also help in cooling rooms without ceilings. Roofs used to be covered with wood shingles, but repeated fires made shingles or sheets of galvanized steel more popular. Also, the latter were more efficient in collecting rainwater for filling the cisterns, the most common source of water supply in the past.

One of the most characteristic features of Key West houses is the decoration used on the facade, especially porches. This millwork was not particularly innovative or a sign of great imagination, as this sort of decorative embellishment was often mass-produced and quite inexpensive. Vine, floral, and interlace patterns were very common, as were spindle balusters and other varieties of gingerbread seen around Key West. At that time one could order an entire prefabricated wooden house by mail, have it delivered to site, and erected by local carpenters. There are a number of houses in Key West which appear to be such houses, but this is difficult to ascertain. In other cases the ornamentation, especially the balusters, are individualized and repre-sent personal or family designs, often indicating the occupation of the owner. There are evidences of at least fifty different patterns of this sort throughout the island. Restoration of older homes often requires special attention to such details and custom-cutting of the patterns.

ARCHITECTUAL
STYLES

I t is fair to call Key Westers conservative when it comes to architecture. Other than the Classical Revival and Vernacular, there are not many pure examples in Key West of the major architectural styles which became popular throughout the rest of the country in the nineteenth century. There is, however, considerable evidence of their presence in the embellishments added over the years to existing structures, which were mostly very simple in design. For instance, although Key West houses are often referred to as Victorian, there are only a few really Victorian houses. Some contemporary formal architectural trends did seep down into Key West, however, so a general review of these styles is in order.

They include the Classical Revival style (an adaptation of the Greek Revival style), the Victorian and Queen Anne styles (with their cousin, the Second Empire style), and two of the Romantic styles—the Gothic Revival and the Italianate. The Romantic styles had little influence in the design of Key West houses. Evidence of them appears mostly in decorative details. Add octagonal to the list as well as the large general group referred to as vernacular, which includes shotgun, and the spectrum of architectural styles represented in Key West is complete. Nineteenth-century Key West houses show little evidence of influence by other major architectural styles popular at that time in the United States. Nineteenth-century Key West architecture is fairly limited in style, homogeneous in appearance and construction, and conservative in design. It is the collection of simple, though decorative, well-proportioned, homes of great dignity that is impressive and appealing. It is this aspect of the houses of Key West that is illustrated in this book.

921 Eaton Street

Most experts would call this house a one-and-a-half-story Classical Revival, but in Key West it is often called a shotgun house. It has classic lines and it is more than the minimal housing associated with shotgun houses. In addition, the usable second story takes it out of the shotgun class. There are no Classical Revival details, however. The porch pillars and balustrades are plain, with only minimal decorative brackets. Its sister house next door is slightly more decorative. The blue color is unusual on Key West houses.

The local term "Conch" originally meant native Bahamian. Nowadays, it refers to native Key Westers and anything else unique to Key West. It is therefore used to describe any typical Key West house. Conch houses are often a mixture of the above styles. Most often, however, it is used to describe houses in the Bahamian style. The term is used loosely and is not a technical one.

Of 855 individual houses in Key West's historic district listed in the Florida Master Site Files, 430 have been classified as Classical Revival, 103 as shotgun vernacular, 18 as Queen Anne, 7 as Gothic Revival, and 3 with mansard roofs (Second Empire). The rest are a variety of other vernacular styles.

CLASSICAL REVIVAL

The Greek Revival period in American architecture lasted from about 1820 to the Civil War, and was the first period in which professional architects became influential. In 1818, William Strickland, one of the earliest American architects of note, introduced the Greek temple style in several public buildings, most notably the Second National Bank of Philadelphia. It was based on the 5th-century B.C. Parthenon in Athens, one of the finest examples of classic Greek architecture. Thomas Jefferson had used this design earlier for the Virginia state capitol building, built in the late 1700s. Other architects used the same model, modifying it to suit Americans' needs for inexpensive and rapid construction using locally available materials.

What soon developed as the typical domestic version of the temple form was

ideally a simple rectangular block of more than one story. It has a low-pitched roof; the main entrance is on the gabled end. The attic story extends beyond the vertical plane of the principal stories, forming a portico. Formal columns (Doric, Ionic, Corinthian, Tuscan) are an integral part of the portico structure. Square pillars are often substituted for columns and crowned with a few simple moldings instead of classical capitals. A plain frieze of smooth boards and a boxed cornice with a few molding strips form a partial entablature. Typically, there is no architrave. A series of small blocks nailed to the soffit board, the board covering the underside of rafters of an overhanging eave, serve as dentils. *(Cultural Survey of Key West,* 1976)

618 Caroline Street

One of the most beautiful Classical Revival temple form houses in Key West, this example is the replacement of the building on this site prior to the fire of 1886. The Sanborn map of 1889 shows a house on this lot. Photographs of the house from the early 1900s show the present facade less some detail in the pediment. It was owned for many decades by various members of the Lawrence Bates family until the 1950s. It was then divided into apartments until it was restored as a single family home in the 1980s. It was purchased by its present owners, Donald and Carol Jo Vecchie, in 1987 in the restored condition it now enjoys.

The distinctive double columns upstairs and down are unique in Key West and similar to the columns on the gallery of the W. Hunt Harris house. The Greek Revival window and door surrounds give this house a formal and dressy appearance. The unusual use of textured concrete block pedestals for the porch supports conflict with the classic features of this house and date it later in the period.

532 Caroline Street
The John J. Delaney House

Above: This four-bay Classical Revival house was built by John J. Delaney after the fire of 1886. In 1862 he married Amelia Elizabeth Lowe, sister of Euphemia Lowe Curry and John Lowe, Jr., and they raised two sons in the house.

One son, Frank, married Sybil Rionette Curry and the other son, William L., married Annie Louise Curtis. Frank and Sybil Delaney occupied the house in the late 1920s. Dr. Edward Gonzales, a physician, lived and practiced in the house in the 1950s and 1960s. It was acquired by the Spottswood family in 1976 and is now occupied by members of the sixth and seventh generations of the Maloney-Bartlum- Spottswood family .

The house was constructed of Charlotte County pine, a wood which is noted for its hardness and termite resistance. The pediment is unusual and graceful in design and its windows unique. Italianate brackets support the cornice, whereas more Victorian ones bracket the first-floor porch pillars. There are bay windows on the side towards the rear of the house.

1017 Fleming Street

Above: The Richard T. Sawyer House was built originally in 1862–1865 at the corner of Southard and Simonton Streets as a one-story house. It was moved to its present location out of town, as the area was considered in earlier days. A storm removed the roof in 1914, and a second story was added. It has served various purposes over the years, such as chapel, music studio, and grocery store. Various members of the Sawyer family occupied the house for over 110 years. It was purchased in 1974 by James Stokes and James Camp, who did a complete restoration over the next couple of years to its present condition. This house is a real Key West original—a Classical Revival with much Queen Anne style decoration, such as spindlework friezes, brackets at each pillar, and delicately turned balustrades. Remnants of its chapel days are attested by a tall stained-glass window in the living room.

527 Fleming Street

Far Left: Temple-form Classical Revival single-family home.

426 Elizabeth Street

Left: This massive four-bay Classical Revival mansion is decorated with mostly Italianate detailing. The unique friezes and porch brackets over the capitals attached mid-height on the pillars are an unusual design, as are the transoms over all the doors and windows. The small door-lights are distinctive. The windows are modern, the balustrades Key West Victorian. Although most of its decoration is Italianate, this house is such a variant that no one style can be chosen for its description.

306 Elizabeth Street
The Old Pirate House

Above: This large Classical Revival mansion has an intriguing history involving pirates and alleged buried treasure. The house was built in 1848 on the site of an old pirates' shack. When the house was restored, the stone piers of the original building were found along with other mementos of pirate days. Local legend told of treasure buried on this block, and offers were made to the owners to move the house so that diggings could be made. It was owned and occupied for many years by the family of Dr. Odet Phillippe, a surgeon in the French Navy and legendary figure in Key West. Apparently he and his family were fleeing from Indian attacks on their plantation in upper Florida en route by ship to Key West when they were captured by the hated pirate, John Gomez. Fortuitously, a tropical fever broke out among the pirates. The doctor offered his services, the men recovered, and Gomez showed his gratitude with a treasure chest and the pirates' shack in Key West. Years later when he moved to the Tampa area and established the first orange grove in Florida, he left the house to his daughter, Charlotte Septima, who married John B. Grillon, a Frenchman. It remained in this family until several years ago.

Its stark, simple lines need no fancy decorations, and only the balustrades place this house in Key West's historic district.

This motif could be seen in almost every nineteenth-century home, church, and town hall in rural New York State and New England. It can still be seen in communities where the economics of real estate has not encouraged the demolition and replacement of older homes. In the deep South, meanwhile, Grecian columns are seen in anything from simple shotgun houses to large mansions. There are Southern houses with enormous Grecian columns on four sides, totally overpowering the boxlike structure which they surround. In some instances you can hardly see the house for the columns.

The term Classical Revival is more apt than Greek Revival to describe most American buildings of this genre. Greek Revival is usually applied only to the architecture designed between 1820–1850 by America's first generation of professional architects. The many anonymous classically inspired structures built later are usually called Classical Revival. This term is thus best applied in Key West where there are almost no classic Greek columns and where this style has been highly modified and adapted to local needs and tastes, and, in the case of the uniquely Key West eyebrow house, a mutant of great dignity and elegance has been created.

Key West Classical Revival houses are usually rectangular, with the roofline either perpendicular (temple style) or parallel to the street. In the latter case they are usually one, or, at the most, two rooms deep, to allow for cross-ventilation.

Floor plans are of two types. In the first type a center hall divides the house into two rooms, each of which might in turn be subdivided. The second type has a side hall arrangement, with the front door to one side of the facade and a hallway through to the back with two or three rooms opening into it.

Every Classical Revival house in Key West has a porch the full width of the facade. Most of these houses have incised porches, that is, cut into the house proper and included under the main roof. In others, the porch roof extends out from the front wall of the house. Temple-form houses have pediments on the gable facing the street but not on the rear facade. The porches are invariably formal and symmetrical. The width is usually three or five bays (the area between columns, usually containing either a door or a window). Side hall

917 Whitehead Street

Left: Decorated with both Victorian and Italianate details, this temple style Classical Revival building is typical of the multi-usage buildings in downtown Key West. It is adaptable either as a two-family residence or as commercial spaces on one or both stories.

719 Fleming Street
The Amos Roberts House

Below: Although this five-bay Classical Revival Conch house has porches on only one facade, it resembles the original Key West Conch houses. (See the description of the Richard Roberts House and the Bahama House.) The ceilings are higher, however.

entrances are commonest in three-bay examples.

One of the most common variations on Key West Classical Revival is the use of slender square columns or pillars instead of classical round columns. In the rare instances when round columns are used, they are usually on the upper gallery over square pillars on the lower. Classical capitals are rarely seen; instead, simple wood moldings are affixed at or near the top of the pillar to give them a classical appearance. Elaborate decorations, suggestive of the Victorian era, are often mixed in.

In the late nineteenth century one could purchase a wide variety of manufactured decorative items—brackets, balusters, handrails, vergeboards, etc. They were added in abundance to Classical Revival houses, contributing to their uniqueness and charm.

EYEBROW HOUSES

One uniquely Key West modification of the Classical Revival style is referred to as the eyebrow house. The author has been unable to locate in the architectural literature any examples of this style in Louisiana, Mississippi, Alabama, Georgia, the Carolinas or elsewhere in Florida. Some architectural historians consider that these houses should really be called hooded houses, since the windows are not eyebrow windows in the technical sense. But the term eyebrow seems to have taken hold.

As the eyebrow house seems to be unique to Key West, one might speculate about its origins. Since the Key West shotgun house is derived from Louisiana, it is logical to look there for the origins of the eyebrow house, also. Indeed, one finds that the most popular American architectural style in Southern Louisiana was the five-bay, one-and-one-half-story galleried center-hall house. These houses often had dormers and gable-end windows, however. Key West eyebrow houses appear to be a variation on this style—certainly the five-bay ones. If one removes the dormers and the ceiling of the gallery, extends the plane of the front facade up to the roof and cuts windows into this area, the result is an eyebrow house. (This holds true for the one-and-one-half-story examples.)

However, some of the Key West eyebrow houses are quite large and have full-height second stories, suggesting the possibility of another origin for this design. The New England saltbox house, in which the front

401 Frances Street

This unusual example is a four-bay asymmetrical version of the eyebrow house, the only one in Key West. (It has three bays upstairs.) The builder must have designed this house to individual taste. The front door is not centered in the porch bay and the porch balustrade extends beyond the pillar in line with the door. The upstairs windows are small. The second floor is a half-story. The brackets are identical to many others around town.

643 William Street
The Edward Roberts House

Left: This Classical Revival eyebrow house is probably the best-known example of this uniquely Key West architectural style on the island. It was designed and built in the 1880s by Edward Roberts, a ship's carpenter. Born in Ireland in 1845, he built the fastest boats in Key West, according to his granddaughter, Mary Euphemia Curry Hinton, who has fond memories of this house. She was the daughter of the only one of seven Roberts children to survive. The house was purchased in 1979 by Lucien and Kathryn Proby, who have lovingly restored and maintained it. Kathryn Proby is a well-known Key West author, best-known for her book on Audubon's sojourn in Florida. Mr. Proby served as judge of the circuit court of Dade County as well as county attorney for Monroe County. This house supports the author's theory of the derivation of the eyebrow house from the New England saltbox house. The front wall of this house is two stories, whereas the rear wall is one. The rear roof slopes down from the ridge to the one-story level, whereas the front roof rests on the porch pillars. The windows of the front two full-height upstairs rooms have been partially obscured by the porch roof, making the eyebrow effect. If the porch roof were removed at its juncture with the front wall,

the house would resemble a New England saltbox house. This is a five-bay center hall house with typical tall, slender pillars supporting the porch roof. However, an atypical feature is the ten-light front door, most likely the only one in town. Most original Key West doors are solid wood, with an occasional one- or two-panelled glass door in turn-of-the-century or later houses. Most likely this door was added at a much later date. The transom above the front door is original, installed by Edward Roberts when he built the house. It is of flash glass—clear glass which has been flashed with rose-colored glass and then hand etched. The process of flashing fuses a thin coating of colored glass on plain glass. The decorative brackets look manufactured and are identical to those on many houses in town. The house was painted blue in the past, but is now a medium gray color. It is one of the most popular houses in Key West, and every Conch Train includes this street on its itinerary.

1121 Southard Street

Above: The yellow color of this five-bay eyebrow house is unusual in Key West. It also has distinctive bracket decorations and a stained-glass transom panel. There is a spiral staircase to a half second story, leaving a cathedral-ceilinged living room.

525 Frances Street

Right: Built in the 1870s by John Roberts, whose family built several eyebrow houses in Key West, and his wife, Rebecca Simonette, this house was nicknamed "hurricane house." Neighbors apparently assembled there for shelter during hurricane weather due to its solidity. It was occupied continuously by the Roberts family until it was purchased and restored in the 1960s by Mr. and Mrs. Lester Morrell. It combines the graciousness of a Southern colonial with the eyebrow design. (There are numerous versions of this house without the eyebrow feature in New Orleans and Southern Louisiana.) Built of virgin pine, with the usual pegs and tongue-and-groove technique, it has elegant classic lines and decorative details. This house looks deceivingly smaller than it is. The windows of the full-height upstairs rooms are unusually obscured by the porch roof.

1415 Truman Avenue

Above: This unusual three-bay eyebrow house has a second-floor gallery with unusual balustrade treatment. One wonders how a grown person could stand on this porch, however.

wall is a two-story vertical plane and the rear wall a one-story plane—the shape of a saltbox—is not unlike the design of the eyebrow house. If this basic design is modified by extending the front roof downwards to rest on columns, forming a porch and creating a permanent, house-width awning over the second-floor windows, the result is again an eyebrow house.

Although this awninglike feature restricts the view from the upstairs windows, it keeps out direct sunlight and has a welcome cooling effect. Removable canvas or metal awnings used in the summer on many other kinds of houses are designed to cover windows to about the same extent as the porch roof in the eyebrow house. Since many of the carpenter-builders of Key West came from New England, it is possible that the eyebrow roof was their modification of a style familiar to them.

VERNACULAR

Vernacular architecture might well be called the architecture of habit. It is the simplest, most straightforward way of building, the result of pragmatism and familiarity, of custom-rooted and oft-times unconscious preference for basic forms and layouts—even on occasion for certain materials and details—that exist independently of passing taste. In the main it is a salient and underlying form or a pronounced and constant feature that distinguishes one folk building-type from another, as well as from more sophisticated and ambitious architectural ventures. Overlaying such forms and features may be the ornamental trappings of this or that architectural style, but stolidly underneath the primary characteristics remain. (Gamble)

The vernacular Key West house, the largest category of residential buildings after the Classical Revival, is a plain structure with few or no decorative details. Construction materials and techniques are the same in each, however. Some are virtually identical to Classical Revival houses except that they lack decorative features such as pillars with capitals, pediments, entablatures, and incised porches. Unlike the Classical Revival, however, porches in the vernacular style are often attached, with the porch roof extending from the front plane of the house. Many vernacular houses are simple rectangular boxlike structures with peaked roofs and porches added on one, two, or three sides. Another common variety of the vernacular resembles the Classic Revival house with roof line parallel to the street and

1305 Newton Street

One-and-a-half-story frame vernacular

40

531 Caroline Street
The John M. Spottswood House

Left: This area was in the path of the fire of 1886. The house is believed to have been built by William Ledwitch, a local merchant, prior to the fire, but only a portion of it was saved. Two new sections were added between 1889 and 1892. The Sanborn Map of 1889 showed no house on this site, but the one of 1892 did. It was later owned and occupied by George L. and Mary E. Bartlum, from whom it was inherited in the 1930s by their grandneice, Florence Maloney (Mrs. Robert) Spottswood. (Dr. John Bartlum Maloney, George Bartlum's uncle, was grandson of Col. Walter Cathcart Maloney, who wrote A Sketch of the History of Key West.*) In the 1940s she gave the house to her son, John M. Spottswood, well-known Key West lawyer and state senator from 1963 to 1965. He married Mary Sellers in 1949 and shortly thereafter they moved into the house and raised three sons and a daughter, two of whom occupy the neighboring Patterson House*

and Delaney House with their families. (See the descriptions of these houses.) Senator and Mrs. Spottswood entertained Harry and Bess Truman in their home during the president's frequent visits to Key West. Mrs. Mary Spottswood continues to occupy the house. Her grandchildren are seventh-generation Conchs. The house is a rather typical frame vernacular T-plan house surrounded by verandas on three sides. The only decorations are the porch balustrades and Classical Revival window and door treatments. There are other houses very similar to this one in Key West.

513 Whitehead Street

Above: Another temple-form downtown multi-usage building with some detailing, this example's commercial look and lack of good design keeps it in the vernacular camp. It has Classical Revival influence and probably resembles many of Key West's early buildings.

incised porch across the street facade, but lacking any decorative details.

SHOTGUN HOUSES

The most important industry in Key West during the 19th-century was cigar-making, employing up to 6000 workers at its peak. Among the most prevalent types of houses in Key West were those built by the cigar factories to house their workers. They constitute the largest category of frame vernacular houses in Key West. For the most part, these houses were of the type known as shotgun houses, so called because the floor plan was of two or more rooms, one behind the other, usually with the successive openings lined up so that if one shot a gun through the front door it would not hit any wall through to the back of the house. In the larger examples, there may be a hallway on the side through to the back.

In Key West these houses vary from the most modest and poorly constructed, usually crowded together on a cigar-factory tract, to larger and well-decorated examples that have been restored and are in great demand as second homes. The more sophisticated examples are difficult to distinguish from frame Classic Revival or vernacular houses of higher quality construction, and can only be identified as shotguns by inspecting the interior floor plan.

Opinions differ as to exactly what defines a shotgun house. Purists confine the term to primarily two-bay folk houses of simple design and construction with little or no embellishment. There are, however, those who prefer a broader definition of the shotgun. One is John Michael Vlach, who states in his doctoral thesis:

> The shotgun house is a one-room wide, one-story high building with two or more rooms, oriented perpendicular to the street with its front door in the gable end. These are the essential features of the shotgun house; they are found in all examples. Other aspects, such as size, proportions, roofing, porches, appendages, foundations, trim, and decoration have been so variable that the shotgun is sometimes difficult to identify. The most important variation in the shotgun is the number of rooms—there can be two to eight or even more. The commonest is three. A notable and distinguishing feature is the placement of the front door. The usual folk house has the door on the long side of the house which is parallel to the street.

821 Frances Street

Meticulously restored three-bay shotgun house with minimal decoration.

Vlach also considers them highly variable in size, even up to 30 feet wide, as one sees in some Key West examples. In Key West, shotguns range from the smallest two-bay minimal versions of the cigar-makers tracts, to the much larger, three-bay individually built examples resembling Classical Revival houses.

In most shotguns, the door is to one side of the facade with the interior doors aligned from one room to the next. However, the larger and more sophisticated ones have a long hallway with the rooms off it to provide more privacy. In any case, one can only identify a shotgun house by inspecting the interior floor plan, as it must have the qualifying alignment of the doors or the hallway through to the rear.

Shotgun houses, like the rest of the island's houses, have no chimneys. They may or may not have a porch, either as a projection from the front facade or incised. Decorations vary, but are not extensive or detailed. Shotgun houses were conceived as minimal housing built as economically as possible. While many of these houses remain in their original condition, many have also been renovated to desirable properties and are in great demand as second homes. Adding modern amenities to these simple houses makes for very comfortable as well as attractive island homes. Key West shotguns vary considerably in size and quality of construction. Most of the smaller shotguns, the real cigar-makers' shacks, were of very poor construction—balloon frame with board and batten siding. Many have been resheathed over the years with a variety of materials, including asbestos shingles.

After the turn of the century, cigar-makers' houses were more commonly constructed out of molded concrete block, which had become available and was more practical. In this period they were built in various styles, shapes, and sizes. Although some were of the shotgun floor plan, more were planned with privacy in mind and came to be classed as bungalows.

Since the shotgun house was the commonest folk dwelling in the South in the nineteenth century, its origin has been the subject of study by architectural historians. One common theory of the origin of the shotgun house is based on the observation that these houses are similar to the trappers' and oystermen's houses of the bayous and other camp-type houses; some even point to earlier American Indian designs.

413 Truman Avenue

This house is one of four in a row (see photo on pp. 50-51) which differ only in window and door treatments. Most probably they were built by one of the cigar factories for rental to employees, the most common origin of shotgun houses in Key West. Some would call this a Classical Revival house, but the lack of classic proportions and the minimal pediment treatment place it in the shotgun camp. This example has been decorated with brackets and door and window surrounds. Since each of this group of four has different detailing, they were probably originally all quite plain and economically built.

620 White Street

Above: Two-bay shotgun house of simple and plain design. It lacks a window for a facade of this width.

822 Olivia Street
Roberts Row Shotgun House

Right: This three-bay shotgun house, together with six others, is in one of the last remaining rows of typical cigar-makers' shacks built in 19th-century Key West. Fernando W. Roberts, local merchant and carpenter, built these houses himself in 1890 for rental to cigar-makers, spongers, and fishermen. Though Roberts was a native Key Wester, his parents were born in Nassau in the Bahamas. All the houses in the row are of identical design and construction but have been individualized with decorative details. Siding is the common board and batten. Porch pillars are minimal, decorations typical, and porch balustrades appear homemade. Hundreds of houses like this one were built in Key West in the 1880s and 1890s.

824 Georgia Street

Far Above: Calling this three-bay sweetheart a shotgun house will undoubtedly invite dispute. Classical Revival and frame vernacular will be mentioned. However, due to its size, the attached porch, and the frequency with which shotguns were enlarged (the second floor looks like an addition), the probability of its having been a shotgun is great. It is not easy to accurately categorize Key West houses like this one.

322 Simonton Street

Above: Three-bay shotgun house with board and batten siding and some hints of Classical Revival detailing.

400 block, Truman Avenue

Left: Four identical shotgun houses with different detailing.

By the late 19th century, shotgun houses were found in almost every small Southern town as well as urban area and were often associated with the black neighborhhoods. As the newly enfranchised blacks became able to afford their own homes, this was their usual dwelling both in urban and rural areas. The area of highest concentration of this type of housing was the lower Mississippi Valley, especially New Orleans and its environs, as well as southern Mississippi and Alabama.

Architectural historian John Michael Vlach has studied the origin of the Louisiana shotgun house and has concluded that it derives from Haiti and before that from West Africa.

1103 Fleming Street

Two-bay shotgun house with Classical Revival style facade, including classic pediment, cornice, capitals, and door and window surrounds. It is more formal than most Key West shotguns. It would be at home in New Orleans.

The shotgun house is thought to have originated in the United States as early as the 1840s in New Orleans, when there was an increasing number of free persons of color in the city who were looking for housing. In New Orleans the predecessor of the shotgun house probably was the Creole cottage, a very popular two-bay, hip-roofed, rectangular structure with the narrow end facing the street. It was the most popular minimal housing style in New Orleans in the 18th and early 19th century in the areas originally inhabited by Creoles and later by freemen. As these houses deteriorated, they were usually replaced by shotguns. Later, in the 1860s, when many blacks migrated from Haiti to New Orleans, the shotgun house again proliferated. Then, from the 1870s through the 1890s, all of New Orleans experienced a great building boom, mostly of the shotgun genre. At this time shotguns were the predominant form of housing for the working man. The houses were either custom-built by individual carpenters or assembled as prefabs.

The wide variety of elaborately decorated shotgun houses in New Orleans makes it the center for the style, and they are often referred to as Louisiana shotgun houses. In New Orleans they vary from two-bay to six-bay, the most frequent of which is the double shotgun, that is, two two-bay houses with a common wall. These have often been opened up later to make a single-family dwelling.

Later, Louisville, Kentucky, and other cities became centers of proliferation of the shotgun style, and even Miami, Florida, had until recently a large area of mostly the Southern shotgun houses. As land values have

612 Elizabeth Street

Left: A typical shotgun house, this example is one room (12 feet) wide and three rooms deep. Originally sheathed in board and batten style, it now has clapboard siding.

608 Angela Street
The Philip Burton House

Above: This is a Victorian "Larry Davis Original," by the well-known Key West builder of the period. He built three similar houses for the three sons of a ship's captain named Johnson, who lived around the corner and wanted his children to be near him. The house was purchased in 1974 by Philip Burton from one of the Johnson granddaughters. Mr. Burton, perhaps the greatest authority on Shakespeare in the world and adopted father of Richard Burton, the actor, lives here in retirement. However, he *remains active in local theater life, giving frequent talks and lectures on his favorite subject. He had the entire house stripped to bare wood, inside and out, and restored it to its present original condition. A front room had been added to this house for use as a hardware store, hence the rather unusual design. The style of this house is "conservative Victorian cottage," conservative because of the very limited decorations. It also resembles the Gothic Revival style, although it lacks the verge-boards, and the roof line is not as steeply pitched as most Gothic Revivals. It is neither fish nor fowl, but a melding of local fashions into another Key West original. Its unpainted state is unusual in Key West, but the richness of the weathered wood attracts much attention. Key West houses are usually painted light colors to reflect the tropical sun.*

increased in cities like Miami, this kind of housing has been largely replaced, while in Louisville, Kentucky, their preservation and restoration is said to have become almost an obsession.

The houses included in this book are mostly larger, three-bay shotguns, since they have been restored in Key West more extensively than the others. Restrictions on restoration in the historic district have preserved the original facades of these modest houses, but it is surprising to see what has been done to some of their interiors. Many have been opened up and contemporized with decks, lush gardens, and pools. In any case, they are interesting examples of Southern vernacular housing of considerable historic and cultural significance as well as charm.

VICTORIAN & QUEEN ANNE

VICTORIAN

Although Queen Victoria reigned from 1837 to 1901, the term Victorian has been applied to the architectural styles popular between 1860 and 1900, the last two decades of which are also referred to as the Queen Anne period. Not many houses in Key West are truly or exclusively Victorian, but many are referred to by this term because of the ornate Victorian decorations added to other basic styles. Mass-produced columns, millwork, and decorative elements associated with Victorian-style houses were widely available and were often added to previously built houses.

703 Fleming Street
A Jerry Herman Victorian
(See description on page 61)

Victorian houses are, for the most part, asymmetrical, with many different planes, extensions, bay windows, porches, and a wide variety of other variations and embellishments. They are subdivided into at least five different sub-types; Queen Anne, Second Empire, Stick, Shingle, and Folk Victorian. Victorian-era houses were often built from plans published in architectural books and decorated and embellished with factory-made items such as windows, doors, balustrades, pillars, brackets, dormers, etc. There were often several different surface textures in the same house, such as clapboard, shingle, brick, stone, patterned brick and stone, patterned wood shingles, etc. There were often different colors on the same house as well.

During the Victorian period great license was taken in using elements from a variety of the picturesque styles, many of which could easily be used interchangeably

with effective results, since highly ornamental was the fashion of the day. Architecturally it was a period of "anything goes." In Key West decorative details were added to making for a potpourri of architectural specimens.

"Folk Victorian," a term used by the McAlesters in their detailed and comprehensive work on house types, offers a description par excellence of many Key West houses:

> The style is defined by the presence of Victorian decorative detailing on simple house forms, which are generally much less elaborated than the Victorian styles that they attempt to mimic. The details are usually of either Italianate or Queen Anne inspiration; occasionally the Gothic Revival provides the source. The primary areas for the application of this detailing are the porch and cornice line. Porch supports are commonly either Queen Anne type turned spindles or square posts with corners beveled (chamfered) as in many Italianate porches. In addition, lace-like spandrels are frequent and turned balusters may be used both in porch railings and in friezes suspended from the porch ceiling. Most Folk Victorian houses have some Queen Anne spindlework detailing but are easily differentiated from true Queen Anne examples by the presence of symmetrical facades and by their lack of textured and varied wall surfaces characteristic of the Queen Anne (McAlesters, 1990).

They consider this a distinct style largely because it makes strong stylistic statements and point out that it was made possible and became popular because of the widespread availability of factory-made decorative items that could be easily transported around the country on railroads. In fact, as one looks around Key West, one sees identical pieces of patterned decorative work on one house after another, indicating mass-production and marketing. Key West houses are really conservative ladies in ornate Victorian clothes.

In Key West examples, the term Folk Victorian is certainly applicable to those Classical Revival and vernacular houses with Victorian details and decoration. This presents a problem in the labelling of these houses, however, which will be left for architectural experts to resolve. Since the term includes a broader range of basic styles than there are in Key West, the current terms, Classic Revival and vernacular, are used in this book.

1311 Truman Avenue
The Jerry Goodman House

This typical Key West Victorian house was built around the turn of the century by Benjamin and Mary Fogarty Trevor. She was daughter of Jeremiah and Rosella Bartlum, one of the many loyalists from England who left the Southern Colonies for the Bahamas and eventually returned to the States via Key West. Mr. Trevor opened the first steam laundry in Key West in the early part of this century and served as the Mayor from 1903-05. The house has seen service as a church, the home of the Womens' Club, as well as private residence.
It was purchased in 1975 by its present owners, Gerald Morgan and Sam Senia, local antique dealers, who did a complete restoration of the house. It was awarded first place by the Old Island Restoration Foundation the first year of the awards. Although it resembles many vernacular houses in Key West, it has predominantly Victorian features. The assymetry of design, the bay windows, the two-pane double-hung windows, the front door, along with the decorative details on the porches are all Victorian. The front door is from the Southernmost house, a gift from its owner.

701 Fleming Street
A Jerry Herman Victorian

Left: Jerry Herman, Broadway producer of La Cage aux Folles, Mame, Hello Dolly, *etc., together with his partner, Marty Finklestein, of Philadelphia, did total restorations of two identical Victorians on Fleming Street. To the left is one of them; the other is picture on page 57. Herman and Finklestein are noted for their restorations of other houses in Key West. The architect for this massive project was Key West's own Tom Pope. The houses are in true Victorian style, with high pitched gables, bay windows, turned balustrades and columns, and multicolored exterior finishing. The interiors have been done in more contemporary style with pale colors, and with a more open feel than most Victorian homes. However, they are conservative like the other Key West Victorian houses.*

323 Whitehead Street
The Banyan House

Above: This conservative Victorian house together with the Cosgrove House next door is part of an interval ownership compound. It has been referred to as "Princess Anne" style. Also known as the Delaney-Holtsburg House, it was built by William Lowe Delaney and his wife Annie Curtis Delaney.

QUEEN ANNE

Toward the end of the Victorian period, from 1880 to 1900, the decorative imagination really went wild, and houses built during that time were referred to as Queen Anne. This style was noted for its verticality, steeply pitched roofs, towers, and multiple porches and galleries. They were usually decorated with much spindlework in the balustrades, gables, friezes, and wherever else possible. These highly decorative embellishments are sometimes referred to as Eastlake, after Charles Eastlake, one of the foremost promoters of elaborate house decorations of the period. Various kinds of columns were used, often double, or even triple, usually rounded, and varying in design, either spindle-shaped or classic. Much bracketing, incised ornamenting, finials, dentils, etc., are in evidence. Most characteristic of the Queen Anne style, however, are the complicated protuberances, breaking of the vertical planes, and extensions from the main house structure—towers, turrets, balconies, dormers, bay windows, overhangs, cantilevered gables, and even partially cantilevered rooms. Particularly characteristic of Queen Anne houses are polygonal or round towers at one corner of the front facade.

The Queen Anne houses in Key West, although they are ornate and show characteristics of the style, in no way even approach the complex, imaginative designs of the true Queen Anne houses found in other parts of the country. Elsewhere, one can find numerous examples of massive, expensive, multileveled and multifaceted, unbelievable conglomerations of every sort of wild architectural elements borrowed from every era since the middle ages.

Apparently in Key West there was neither the sophistication nor the great wealth required to conceive and subsidize such architectural monstrosities. Only one

313 William Street
The George A. Roberts House

Right: This rare Key West Queen Anne specimen has been faithfully restored and brought back to life. The corner tower with hexagonal roof-cap, the multiple porches, room extensions, and highly decorative millwork friezes places this house squarely in the Queen Anne period. The millwork is probably unique to this house. It lacks the texture variations usually associated with the Queen Anne style, however.

708 Eaton Street
The William Russell House

Left: Not much is known about this house. It is named for William Russell, who was well known as the owner of the Russell House, a large hotel built on the site of the older Jefferson Hotel. The house has been owned and occupied in recent years by Windle Davis and Dini Lamot, well-known contemporary rock stars, and is popular with house tours. There is a large wood-panelled ballroom and an enormous pool in the rear made from an old cistern. The architectural style of this house is mixed. The central pedimented gable with wings is reminiscent of the Gothic Revival, but without the usual steepness of the roofline and the vergeboards. The five-bay Classical Revival porch and the Victorian balustrades and porch brackets are both distinctive features calling out to name the house style, also.

house in Key West, the Milton Curry Newport Cottage-style mansion, might be called high style Queen Anne. Also, since architectural preferences are influenced by local customs and environmental needs, such large houses were not suited to the tropics, where good ventilation is important, frequent painting and termite control are required, and hurricanes are common. The few Queen Anne houses in Key West are relatively conservative examples and show only some features of the style.

SECOND EMPIRE

Second Empire, another very popular style of the 19th-century, has no typical examples in Key West. This style is most noted for the mansard roof, popular in France during the period of Napoleon III (1852-70) and in this country between 1860 and 1880. During this period, certain elements of the style were used in remodelling a few Key West houses, most notably, the Dr.J.Y. Porter House and the Hemingway house.

The most typical characteristic of the Second Empire style was the roof line, which was almost vertical and allowed for full head room in the top story, adding useful space on that floor. Also typical were the under-eaves brackets, reminiscent of the Italianate-style; central towers, either square or rectangular; as well as dormers and elaborate detailing in the windows, also in the Italianate-style.

GOTHIC REVIVAL

Gothic Revival, popular in America from 1840 to 1880, is poorly represented in the South in general, and in Key West in particular. In the 19th century professional architects came into their own, and in attempts to popularize their particular leanings they championed several distinct styles. Gothic Revival style originated in England in the mid-18th century and was introduced in this country by the architects Alexander Jackson Davis and Andrew Jackson Downing.

The Gothic Revival style is characterized by steeply pitched roofs, usually side gabled with highly decorated vergeboards. The facade walls usually extended into the gables, as did the pointed arched windows. There was usually a one-story porch with Gothic decorations, arches, and pillars. Only one house in Key West, the Kerr house on Simonton Street, can be considered true Gothic Revival. However, as the *Key West Cultural Survey* notes, "it is basically a cottage in the Classical Revival style. Its 'gothicism' lies in the quatrefoils above the columns on the U-shaped veranda and the tracery motif found in the balustrade surrounding the small balcony in the gable above the veranda and in the vergeboard. The pointed arch is nowhere to be seen." Only a few houses in Key West show elements of the Gothic Revival style, mostly in the roof line. This is another example of what happened in Key West: Features of a formal architectural style were appropriated but there was no attempt to produce a complete classic example of the style.

ITALIANATE

Just like the Gothic Revival, this style, popular in the North between 1840 and 1885, was not popular in the South during the Reconstruction. The Italianate style was seen more in urban areas, where land was scarce. Like Gothic Revival, it was popularized by Andrew Jackson Davis, but with the financial panic of 1873, both these styles lost appeal, and by the time building was again in full swing, the Victorian influence had taken over. Consequently, very few examples of this style, if any, were built in Key West. However, there are Italianate details and embellishments on houses built in other styles here and there around town.

The characteristic features of this style are the wide overhanging roof eaves, very low-pitched roof, and prominent brackets under the eaves. A square cupola usually tops the roof, and windows and doors usually have inverted U-shaped crowns and other very elaborate pediments. The latter are seen in some larger houses in Key West, especially the J.Y. Porter House and W. Hunt Harris House.

OCTAGONAL STYLE

Although there are very few examples in the country of the multifaced-style houses, referred to mostly as octagonal (even though there can also be 6, 10, or 12 sides), there are at least two remaining in Key West. They are not true octagonal houses, however, since they only have multifaced extensions and some would describe them as bowed houses.

410 Simonton Street
The William Reid Kerr House

William Reid Kerr was one of the foremost 19th-century builders in Key West. Born in County Kerr, Ireland, in 1836, he came to United States as a teenager and arrived in Key West with the Union Army just prior to the Civil War. He built this house for himself in the 1870s and married Emma Russell in the almost completed home. In 1878 his daughter, Ida Kerr Hayes, wife of Dr. John B. Hayes, was born. Mr. Kerr also built the Convent of Mary Immaculate and the First Methodist Church (Old Stone), as well as the Florida National Bank building. He also built the Julius Otto house next door. The Kerr house is the closest thing in Key West to the "carpenter gothic" style, which was just becoming popular in the rest of the country at that time. Alexander Downing published his book with illustrations of a variety of house patterns and plans and with it began the period of popularity of elaborate decorative embellishments. Many of the decorations like those seen in this house could be purchased from factories which proliferated due to the newly developed rail transport system. Mass-produced products could be shipped all over the country. However, Key West could only be reached by boat at that time, so there was a delay in the arrival of contemporary styles on the island. These houses were already quite popular and sprouting up all over the country, especially on the East Coast. The decorations are coarser than the lacy ones seen in Classical Revival Key West homes. They were more often than not individually made.

GREAT HOUSES

Of all the houses of Key West, there are a certain few that stand out for reasons of size, design, uniqueness, historical interest, and any prominent personalities involved. Oftentimes houses have been named for their original owners, and in other cases after subsequent owners, especially if they have achieved some prominence in Key West. Key West families are often quite closely connected. Intermarriages among certain prominent families have been frequent, so that certain names reappear in relation to several of these houses.

Some of the information for this section has been culled from historical works, such as the Browne history, while some has been acquired directly from present owners and relatives of former owners. Numerous magazine and newspaper articles have been written about individual Key West houses and there is a large collection of clippings in the historical section of the Monroe County Library in Key West. Many of these articles have been occasioned by the annual house tours of the Old Island Restoration Foundation.

Seventeen great houses of Key West are featured here. There are other eligible houses still standing in town that could be included in this group, and there were other distinguished houses that are no longer in existence. We have here chosen the most photogenic, interesting and well-known of the remaining great houses of Key West.

THE JOHN LOWE, JR. HOUSE
620 Southard Street

This impressive house was built in 1855 by John Lowe, Jr., son of a well-known Key Wester who made a fortune as a wrecker. The Lowe family was one of the first to migrate to Key West from the Bahamas in the 1830s. This prominent Key West family has figured widely in the history of the island, and the name comes up frequently in a discussion of the island's history, commerce, and culture.

John Lowe, Jr., was born in the Bahamas and came to Key West shortly after his birth. He had a varied career. He was a wrecker like his father at first, but soon went out on his own, working as a clerk with the Bowne and Curry firm—which later became William Curry and Sons, the largest mercantile house on the island. In 1878 he went into business on his own and eventually made his fortune as the owner of a fleet of sponge and lumber ships. He was also renowned as the owner of the the sailing ship, *Magic*, winner of the America's Cup race in 1870.

Occupied by members of the Lowe family until 1945, the house has served in various functions over the years since then. During World War II it served as a canteen for the USO, and later in the 1940s was used by Dr. J.Y. Porter II

as a hospital. It was subsequently broken up into separate apartments and used as a multiple residence. It was restored to its original condition by Mr. and Mrs. Griscom Bettle, of Philadelphia. As with most Key West houses, deterioration proceeded and it was again completely redone by its present owners in the 1980s.

Built of heart pine and Honduran mahogany, it is perhaps the finest example of the Classical Revival Bahaman style on the island. It was selected by the Historical American Buildings Survey in 1967. It was originally a one-story house, but another story and a half was later added, with verandas on three sides, upstairs and down. Built in the old tradition, it was constructed with wooden pegs, mortise-and-tenon joints, and square timbers. Of special note are the slender two-story square columns to which the upper porch is attached, rather than the usual one-story columns on top of each other.

It is a large and spacious mansion, with 12-foot ceilings and only a few very large rooms off the typical central hall. It has one of the few remaining widow's walks in Key West. Actually, these were not widow's walks at all. There were many in Key West at one time, and their primary use was as lookout stations for wreckers. The first one to reach a wreck had the great advantage of being in charge of the operation, so there was great competition amongst the wreckers to sight and set off for a wreck first. John Lowe, Jr., was in the wrecking business for a while and probably made good use of this vantage point on his rooftop.

The heavy growth of trees and plantings on the Lowe house property now practically obscures the view of the house itself, but the overall effect is one of lush elegance unequaled on the island. It is one of Key West's most beautiful landmarks and should not be missed by visitors to the island. The house is painted a rather pale rose color— not the color used in the original decades of its existence, as most houses in town were white with green or black shutters. Its simple lines have no Victorian decorations and need none; consequently, the house has a more Caribbean appearance than most other houses in town.

THE W. HUNT HARRIS HOUSE
425 Caroline Street

In 1896, Dr. J.Y. Porter (see also the J.Y. Porter House) and his wife, Louisa Porter, nee Curry, gave their oldest daughter, Mary Louise, a wedding present of the land next door to their own stately home when she married W. Hunt Harris. The young Harris had come to Key West from Louisiana after the death of his father while he was studying medicine at Tulane University. Unable to continue his studies, he was invited to move to Key West by his uncle, Dr. Jeptha Vining Harris, the collector of customs in Key West. The uncle persuaded Harris to read for the law while earning his living as a lighthouse keeper. In those days one didn't necessarily have to attend formal law school, but could study independently and then pass the bar exams. This Harris did after he had saved enough money to travel to Tallahassee, a long overland trip in those days.

He soon opened a law practice in Key West; the going was rough, so he worked as a cigar-maker on the side to help pay the bills. He became interested in politics and started in public service as police justice. In 1898 he was elected to the Florida House of Representatives and later to the Florida Senate, where he was its president, the lieutenant governor, from 1907 to 1909. Returning to Key West he became judge of the Criminal Court. Of course, he was now in one of the prominent families in town, his wife being the granddaughter of William Curry. The Curry family was one of the oldest and most well-known families of Key West, one of the first to have migrated from the Bahamas in the 1830s.

The Harrises began construction of the house as the Spanish-American War broke out but apparently couldn't finance its completion. When the navy came to town, maximal facilities were needed in a hurry. They offered to take over the property, along with many others on the island, and complete its construction for use as offices for the duration. After the war, in about 1904, the Harrises completed the house to their satisfaction and moved in.

The house was designed by Frank P. Milburn, a prominent architect from the Carolinas. It is probably one of the few houses in Key West to have been designed and built under the supervision of a well-known architect.

The house was occupied by a succession of members of the

Harris family until 1976 when it was sold by to Messrs. Martin and Dodd, who began a restoration of the property. It turned out that a second house had been moved onto the property and merged with the original in order to make a two-family building. The house was used subsequently as offices for a few years by Mel Fisher's Treasure Salvors, Inc.

Purchased by its present owner in 1982, it has undergone a complete and rather spectacular restoration, so that it is now one of the real showplaces of Key West. It was found to have been constructed of the highest quality wood and materials. The interior of the house was entirely dismantled and rebuilt into a large one-family home with all modern amenities, such as central air-conditioning. The front porch and gallery design was duplicated on the rear facade of the house, overlooking the garden area.

In Key West, house styles are usually a mixture of what was currently popular together with practical considerations of climate and availability of materials. This house has a high-peaked Gothic-style roof over a Classical Revival portico with four graciously arched bays—a mixed design, though there are other houses quite similar in town. The porch columns are square, panelled, and chamfered in the Italianate style, whereas those on the gallery upstairs are double, round, and Tuscan, more reminiscent of the Classical Revival. The balustrades are round, lathe-turned, characteristic of Victorian decoration. The exquisite front door treatment, a geometrically perfect hemispherical arch, is quite distinctive and rare in Key West. With its paired doors with large-pane glazing, it most resembles doors in the Italianate or Second Empire style.

There is an array of outdoor living spaces surrounding a rather large pool. What had been an outdoor kitchen has been converted into an outdoor living room. The Tuscan column motif is carried out in this building, the uncovered portion of which extends onto a platform carefully cut to fit snugly around an enormous sapodilla tree. An open dining area decorated with latticework overlooks the pool, and several seating areas are spaced around the tastefully landscaped rear yard. The total restoration took four and a half years to complete. The project was planned and executed under the direction of the designer, Richard Motley, together with the firm of Michael Rubin, New York architect, with the assistance of the project engineer, Joseph Kluczinsky, and the Key West master-carpenter, Glen Gauthier.

THE FREEMAN-CURRY HOUSE
724 Eaton Street

The imposing Freeman-Curry House, as it is now known, was built in 1865 by Samuel Filer and remained in the family until the 1920s when it was purchased by T. Jenkins Curry and his wife, Muriel Louise Thompson, of Green Turtle Bay and Marsh Harbor in the Bahamas. He was descended from the well-known Curry family, Loyalists who fled from the Carolinas to the Bahamas during the American Revolution and were rewarded with a land grant in the Bahamas from Charles III. Mr. Curry was in business in Key West and served as county commissioner from 1938 to 1940.

The Currys completely remodeled the house in the 1920s, moving it back forty feet from the street to its present location with the help of mules, logs, a windlass, and a banyan tree in the backyard as anchor. The outdoor kitchen and outhouse were replaced with additions to the main building. The house was built of Dade County pine—the walls, floors, and ceiling. (Due to a high resin content, this wood is virtually impervious to the ubiquitous Key West termites.) However, in the 1920s pine panelling was not in style, so the walls were covered over with beaverboard, a popular decorative material of the era. A well-known Key West artist, Joaquin Barroso, was commissioned to decorate the walls of the large livingroom-ballroom with oil paintings; he covered the walls with landscapes of scenes from the owner's life—one on top of the other. The room looks much like an art museum.

The house was later occupied by the Currys' daughter, Eloise, and son-in-law, William Freeman, Sr., who was active in local politics, serving on the Key West City Council from 1927 to 1944. They raised their two sons, David and William, Jr., in the house.

The house was subsequently owned by William Freeman, Jr., who occupied it throughout his lifetime. Mr. Freeman was very active in politics, serving as county commissioner for a record twenty years from 1954–1974, and as state representative from 1974–1976. However, he was best known for his thirteen years of service as Monroe County Sheriff from 1975–1988. Dr. Shirley Freeman, his wife, is the present owner and occupant.

Built in the Classical Revival style, the house typifies the large mansions of the Gulf states and also shows the influence of the Bahamas, as do many houses in Key West.

Elms Court in Natchez, Mississippi, dating from 1836, is almost identical in design except for the lacelike ironwork added to the latter in the 1850s. This house could be at home in any of the Southern states or the Bahamas, and yet, together with its distinctive and varied decorative elements is quite characteristically Key West Conch at its very best. There are under-eaves brackets in the Italianate style, which, together with the other decorative elements, are in

contrast to the rather plain and formal Classical Revival window and door surrounds. However, the transom and paired doors with glazed panels are also Italianate. This mixture of styles is common in Key West. The transom and front door panes are of red cranberry glass etched with a grinding wheel, the kind of glass used in lighthouses of the period. The balustrades and corner brackets on the lower porch are identical to those on the J.Y. Porter House described elsewhere. No doubt they were manufactured and available generally—although many of these decorations were custom made for a particular house.

THE E.H. GATO, JR., HOUSE
1327 Duval Street

This lovely, large, frame vernacular Conch mansion was built by Edward Hidalgo Gato for his son, E.H. Gato, Jr., in about 1885. The senior Gato was one of the original cigar manufacturers who migrated from Cuba at the time of the revolt in the late 1860s. Originally, the house was on the north side of Duval Street, with the main porch facing south. Mr. Gato soon found out that the porch was too hot for comfort, so he moved the house across the street by mule-power to its present location, facing north. The house number was never changed and remains the only odd-numbered house on that side of Duval Street.

The senior Gato was a very prominent local entrepreneur. Aside from owning one of the largest and most highly regarded clear-Havana cigar factories in the United States, in 1885 he financed a company formed to start a mule-drawn streetcar line, which he then built and operated. He was also quite civic-minded, and when a group of local citizens established a hospital, which they named the Casa del Pobre, Mercedes Hospital, he donated his former home rent-free for a number of years for its quarters. It was named in honor of his wife, Mercedes.

The house remained in the Gato family until the 1930s when it was sold to Eugene Martinez. It was subdivided into rental apartments and remained so until it was sold again in 1987 to Ramona Santiago, the present owner, who operates the premises as the Southernmost Point Guest House.

As for architectural description of this house, the extensive millwork and other decorative details are conspicuously Queen Anne. The delicately turned balustrades, the spindle-work friezes, the complicated corner brackets with spindles, the turned double and triple porch supports are all characteristic of this style. The double pillars up and down are quite unusual in Key West, although common in Queen Anne houses elsewhere in the country. The roof is pyramidal, whereas the facade resembles the Italianate model. Outside staircases, two-story verandas, bay windows, and multiple galleries added to rear extensions make for a complicated design typical of the Queen Anne period. Overall, it is vernacular Conch, a Key West adaptation of a mixture of familiar styles, with a variety of embellishments.

THE BARTLUM-FOGARTY HOUSE
718 Eaton Street

Also known as the Joseph Bartlum house, the front section of this two-story house was originally constructed in the Bahamas and brought over on a raft by Joseph Bartlum when he emigrated to Key West. He had purchased several lots in the area, one of which he sold to his brother, John, and another to Richard "Tuggy" Roberts, both of whom also brought houses from the Bahamas to Key West. (See also the Bahama House and the Richard Roberts House.) Building materials were scarce in Key West and these men had built their homes in the Bahamas of fine woods such as madeira mahogany, cypress, and teak, which they had accumulated from salvaged ships. They wanted to keep their prized houses, so they disassembled them and shipped them to Key West with the rest of their belongings. These were tight houses— built like furniture—and amenable to this sort of treatment.

Joseph Bartlum was married to Mary Lowe, daughter of John and Mary Ann Curry. The house was later occupied by the Bartlum's daughter, Rosella, who married Jeremiah Fogarty; hence the house was known as the Fogarty house for many years. Jeremiah Fogarty became prominent in Key West, and at different times was a merchant, U.S. customs official, banker, and general manager of William Curry and Sons. The Fogartys raised two sons and a daughter in the house. Joseph became a physician and mayor of Key West and owned the well-known Fogarty House on Duval Street. Another son, Charles, became a dentist and ran the town pharmacy, while Grace, their daughter, married Stephen Lowe, son of John Lowe, Jr., builder of the Lowe house on Southard Street.

Members of the Bartlum-Fogarty family owned the property until 1950, when it was sold by the heirs to the Paul Millers. The new owners, during an extensive restoration of the house, found typical evidence of early construction methods of ships' carpenters, such as mortise-and-tenon joints, wooden pegs, and the like. The ceilings of this house are of mahogany and teak, the floors of pine, and the walls of cypress. During restoration, barnacles were found clinging to the beams, suggesting that the front part of the house was actually floated over from the Bahamas. The hand-sawn balustrades and brackets are Victorian, but the windows look almost modern in their slender, simple design. There is a pool in the rear, built in what was once a cistern.

THE DR. J. Y. PORTER HOUSE
429 Caroline Street

The earliest information about this massive, emerald "grande dame" of a mixed-style mansion dates to 1837 when the land was sold by a Mr. Green to Judge James Webb, of Georgia, who was commissioned first judge of the newly designated Superior Court of Key West in 1828. He built the house in Virginian style and lived there until he retired from the bench and moved to Texas in 1838 where he became secretary of state of that republic before its admission to the union.

The house was subsequently owned and lived in by several families until it was purchased in 1845 by Joseph Y. Porter, of Charleston, South Carolina. He married Mary Ann Randolph, daughter of Capt. Thomas Mann Randolph, but died at the early age of 32, leaving one son, who was to become one of Key West's most illustrious citizens, Dr. Joseph Y. Porter. Dr. Porter was born in 1847 in the same room in this house in which he died in 1927. His mother died in 1860 at age 30, leaving him to be raised by his grandmother, Susan Brown Randolph. He spent some of his teenage years in Burlington, New Jersey, with her. The young Porter went on to study medicine at Jefferson Medical College in Pennsylvania, graduating in 1870. He then served nineteen years in the Army Medical Corps, during which time he was stationed as acting assistant surgeon at Fort Jefferson in the Dry Tortugas, where the famous Dr. Mudd was imprisoned for treating John Wilkes Booth after the Lincoln assassination.

When the Florida State Board of Health was organized in 1889, Dr. Porter became its first state health officer and was considered one of the foremost experts on sanitation and yellow fever in the United States. He married Louisa Curry, oldest daughter of William Curry, who had come to Key West from the Bahamas in 1847, a member of one of the original families to come to Key West from the Bahamas. This was a merging of two of the oldest names and most prominent of Key West families—the Currys and the Porters. Dr. Porter made his name as a famous physician, and William Curry, when he died in 1896, was considered the richest man in Florida.

Dr. Porter's son, William Randolph Porter, also became a prominent citizen, amassing large real estate holdings in Key West. His daughter, Jessie Porter Newton, better known as Miss Jessie, was active in local affairs, especially in the restoration and preservation of the historic homes in Key

West. One of the original founders of the Old Island Restoration Foundation, she spent over 25 years fighting to save and preserve the old houses. It was Miss Jessie who had the house painted emerald green. She felt that white was a good color for up north where the winter weather was bleak.

In Key West she wanted the houses to reflect the surrounding sea. The Porters had several houses on the street and she had them all painted various shades of green. She also wanted the trim white to suggest whitecaps. (The Carey House, described next is painted a rather pale blue-green shade in contrast to the Porter House's darker emerald shade.)

The house passed on to Dr. Porter and in 1896 he and his wife, Louisa, restored and remodeled it extensively. They added the third floor with the present mansard roof and many closely set dormers for optimal ventila-tion, several small balconies with fancy wrought-iron decorations, along with lots of Victorian trim, making for quite a conglomeration of architectural styles. Porches were also added in the rear, which have subsequently been enclosed. This is one of the very few examples of Second Empire architecture in Key West, primarily because of the mansard roof, the third-floor dormers, and under-eaves brackets. It is similar to the Italianate style, but with less overhang of the eaves. The window, door, and dormer surrounds are also in the Italianate style.

This house is one of the better examples of how in Key West a very plain, classical house has been altered in the fashion of the day and completely transformed into an entirely different architectural style. In this case, however, Key West lagged behind the rest of the country, as the Second Empire style was most popular in the United States between 1860 and 1880. By the time this house was redone, it had already gone out of fashion elsewhere. (It had never been very popular in the South.) The house had few rooms, but they were all quite large. It was subdivided into apartments on the upper floors and commercial spaces below, and it continues in this multiple-usage today.

The house is now owned by Dr. Porter's great-granddaughter, Jeane Porter, and her three children. One of Miss Jessie's daughters, she has spent the last forty-odd years looking after the house and maintaining it in its present excellent condition.

HERITAGE HOUSE
410 Caroline Street

This magnificent Classical Revival Conch mansion was built about 1837 by Capt. George Carey, an Englishman of some distinction who claimed direct lineage from William the Conqueror and who made a fortune in the wholesale and retail "spirits" business in early Key West. "He was a handsome, ruddy white-bearded Englishman, an ex-sailor, and said to be of a good family: in his cups he was wont to boast that his 'ancestors could write on paper without lines on it'" (Browne, 1914).

Originally there had been a small two-room house that was moved back to make way for the present one, which was built with two stories and attic. Since then here have been modifications and additions to the house. Rooms were added to accommodate expanding families. A major remodelling and restoration was done in the 1930s by Mr. and Mrs. Wallace Kirke. Mrs. Kirke was also known as Miss Jessie and later Mrs. Jessie Porter Newton. (See description of the Dr. J.Y. Porter house.) The roof was raised to make a full third floor and porches were added on two levels. The dining room doors were salvaged from the Royal Palm Hotel in Palm Beach. All the windows on the front facade are Dutch doors, split in the middle for use as windows or doors for better ventilation and easy access. The work was done by Mr. Kirke and a well-known local carpenter, Joe Shadrack Meshack Abednego Hannibal. Also known as the Capt. George Carey House, it was lovingly nurtured back to its former glory and furnished with antiques of the period by the Kirkes. This house was the first house included on the Old Island Days house tours.

The Kirkes were very active socially and in local affairs, and Miss Jessie was later one of the original founders of the Old Island Restoration Foundation. During the thirties and forties she more or less held court in the tropical garden of Heritage House, entertaining many illustrious figures of the day who visited Key West, especially those in the literary, philosophical, theater, and art worlds. A cottage in the garden is called the Robert Frost Cottage, in which the poet stayed on numerous occasions. Such luminaries as John Dos Passos, Ernest Hemingway, John Dewey, Tennessee Williams, Vincent Price, Gloria Swanson, Elmer Davis, and many others were frequent visitors, along with Sally Rand, the fan dancer, a very popular member of the ever-changing, always interesting group. Miss Jessie was the Pearl Mesta of Key West and invitations to her gatherings were highly valued. Like the J.Y. Porter house, Heritage House is painted blue-green, but of a lighter shade, in keeping with Miss Jessie's desire to reflect the color of the surrounding seas in her houses. It is now owned and occupied by Jeane Porter, Miss Jessie's daughter, who is also very active in the restoration movement in Key West and a familiar figure on the island. She has maintained the house over the years and it is her plan that Heritage House will be developed as a cultural center and living history museum, as its antique-filled rooms are spacious, the lo-

cation excellent, and its historic significance obvious.

The house is a prime example of a Classical Revival Conch style in the best tradition with a most elegant and gracious design. This house shows some of the more characteristic features of the Classical (Greek) Revival style: the wide cornice of the main roof, the plain capitals on the square columns, the very plain window surrounds, and the door surround. The latter consists of side panels of small glass panes and a three-paned, stained-glass transom—very typical in Classical Revival houses. Decorative items are more varied—the very plain porch balustrades, the decorative dentils, and the Italianate under-eaves brackets. This inconsistency in styles attests to a history of repeated remodelling of the house at varous times over the 150-odd years of its life. (The interior decor and furnishings range from Early American through mid-century African, and much in between.)

THE COSGROVE HOUSE
321 Whitehead Street

The property on which this lovely Classical Revival Style house sits was part of the land which John Whitehead sold in 1829 to P.C. Greene, one of the four original proprietors of Key West. The original one-story house was built in 1850 by a man named Lord. Not much more is known about the house except that it changed hands a few times until it was purchased in 1871 by Capt. Philip. L. Cosgrove, Jr., and his wife, Josephine, for $1,600. Capt. Philip L. Cosgrove, Sr., served in the light-house service until 1906 and commanded the U.S lighthouse tender *Mangrove*, the first ship to leave Key West to rescue the victims of the *Maine*. His son, Philip L. Cosgrove, Jr., born in 1871 and known as Bub, took over his father's command in the lighthouse service after attending Gainesville College. He subsequently had command of a series of ships on duty from Maine to Puerto Rice, and was a warrant officer in the navy during the Spanish-American War, in command of the *Mangrove* when she captured the Spanish prize vessel *Panama*.

Upon the death of Capt. Cosgrove, Sr., the property passed to his son and also to his daughter, Emma R. Arnold. It remained in the Cosgrove family until 1947, when it was purchased by Mr. and Mrs. William Gamble. The new owners prized the house, filled it with antiques of the period, and opened it to house tours for all to appreciate. More recently the house has been acquired by commercial owners and together with the neighboring Banyan House, is part of an interval ownership resort compound.

A second story and attic stretching the full length of the house were added to accommodate the Cosgroves' growing family. Structural features of note in this house are the 16-inch square hand-hewn foundation beams fastened with wooden pegs, the extra thick chestnut floorboards on the porch, the square rooms with high ceilings, and oversized windows and doors—all adaptations for the tropical climate of Key West. A cistern was found under the flooring in which fish were kept to keep out the mosquitoes and keep the water fresh.

The tremendous rubber tree (*Ficus elastica*) in the front yard was planted by Myrtle Cosgrove, wife of Philip L. Cosgrove, Jr., from cuttings brought over from somewhere in the Caribbean by her ship's captain husband.

The Southernmost House
1400 Duval Street

Perhaps the most famous and well-known of Key West's historic houses, this lovely example of a Queen Anne variation on the Victorian theme was built in 1900 by Judge Jeptha Vining Harris. Judge Harris married into another prominent family when he married Florida Curry, the youngest daughter of William Curry. He was also cousin to W. Hunt Harris, who was married to Marie Louise Porter, daughter of Louisa Curry Porter, Florida's sister.

It is said that the house was originally sheathed in dark red brick of the type then used for street paving, but when Florida returned from a trip abroad, she was displeased with the look of the place and insisted that the entire house be covered with the present cream-colored brick, which had to be shipped over from New Orleans. The walls are two and one-half feet thick. It is also said that Judge Harris feared attacks by Seminole Indians, who had once inhabited the area, so he had one of the very few excavated basements in Key West dug as a shelter. Reputedly, there are secret passageways from most of the rooms of the house leading to this shelter in case of a surprise attack. It is doubtful that it was ever used for this purpose, however.

Over the years the house has changed hands and had a variety of usages. During the 1940s it was a gambling club of some notoriety, the Casa Cayo Hueso Club, where many notables, including Walter P. Chrysler, spent a lot of time and money. He is alleged to have built a waterside beach house on the property for his use. It then became the private home of Hilario and Placeres Ramos. Their two children, Charles and Mathilde, grew up in this house and they are the present owners of the property. Mathilde has remained in residence and is actively restoring parts of the house in need of attention in order to keep this magnificent symbol of old Key West in its original condition.

Mr. Ramos is noted for his election to the state legislature when, in 1961, at the age of 24 years, he unexpectedly defeated the incumbent, Bernie C. Papy, who had long been the so-called "boss" of Key West. Mr. Papy had held the position for a long time, was very powerful in the county, and was considered by most to be undefeatable. Mr. Ramos had already served as Monroe County Commissioner as well as mayor of Key West in his early twenties. In the late 1950s, Mr. Ramos, along with the famous "Miss Jessie" Porter Newton, was instrumental in starting the restoration of the historic homes of Key West. In fact, restorations of the Southernmost House and the Audubon House were the first really authentic restoration projects in town.

Some will say that it is no longer the truly "southernmost" house, as two other houses have been built between it and the southernmost point. But because its property originally included all the land involved, it is still considered the Southernmost house and probably always will be.

The variations in color, shapes, textures and sheathing materials along with the decorative embellishments, the

towers, dormers, and galleries, are all characteristic of the Queen Anne style. The porch balustrades, round, double columns, decorative window surrounds, dentils, and brackets all add to the effect. It is one of the few multi-colored houses in Key West. Although it is probably the best-known example of the Queen Anne style in Key West, it is a relatively conservative and formal example of this style.

The house is a good illustration of the fact that Key West Queen Anne houses do not compare in complexity of design, variation in materials, and complication of execution and construction with other elaborate Queen Anne houses elsewhere around the country. As is the case with most of the Key West examples of formal architectural styles, the influence is usually not carried out completely but exhibits elements of that style adapted to local tastes and usage. For Key West, however, this house will always be a point of interest and evidence that Key West is part of the United States and knew the current fashions.

The Southernmost House has been a subject for many local artists, most notable of whom is Robert Kennedy. Mr. Kennedy, artist and owner of a number of art galleries in Key West and the East Coast, has done numerous renderings of this house including sketches, etchings, and watercolors.

THE BAHAMA HOUSE
730 Eaton Street

Perhaps the most authentically Bahamian house in Key West is this one, which was originally built in Abaco, disassembled there, brought over on a schooner by Captain John Bartlum in 1847 and rebuilt on the outskirts of town before the streets were in place. He was the son of John and Mary Curry Bartlum and brother of Joseph, who sold him the land on which the house is located. (See the description under the Bartlum-Fogarty House above.) As another typical example of the family ties in Key West, John Bartlum married Sarah Lowe, daughter of William and Eliza Albury Lowe. William Lowe, who married Mary Ann Curry, was brother to John Lowe who had also migrated to Key West from the Bahamas. (See the descriptions of the John Lowe, Jr., House and the Freeman-Curry House.)

Capt. Bartlum was a native of Green Turtle Bay in the Bahamas and a descendent of a loyalist family, many of whom settled there at the time of the American Revolution. Of Scotch-Irish descent, they had originally settled in South Carolina. He was considered a mechanical genius and gained a wide reputation as a shipbuilder. He became known for building large schooners, one of which, the *Euphemia*, was made for Mr. William Curry and named after Mrs. Curry. It was a huge success, and was later sold for use in the slave trade between Cuba and the coast of Guinea. His work be-came so renowned that he was commissioned to build the first and only clipper ship to be built in Florida, the *Stephen R. Mallory*. Named after another Key Wester, who was a United States Senator from Florida and later Secretary of the Navy of the Confederacy, the ship was said to have been built entirely of madeira mahogany.

Bartlum's fame in shipbuilding spread, but he declined further commissions in order to end his days in Key West. He had a large family, many distinguished in their careers. One of his sons, George L. Bartlum, was mayor of Key West three times.

This house was one of two transported from the Bahamas, the other being the Richard "Tuggy" Roberts house next door. At the time the streets were not in place, and though John Bartlum placed his two porches facing east and west, Roberts faced his north and south, guessing the street would be placed to his advantage. When the streets were laid out, the Roberts house faced sideways, but the Bartlum house was on the corner with one porch facing the street. He later moved the other porch to face the street, making an L-shaped veranda. The porches in these houses are technically verandas, as they are cut under the roof of the house and extend around the corner to a second side. Originally there were stairs outside on the porches, but they were moved inside during a restoration in 1962. The original floor plan was of the typical center-hall-through of Bahama houses. It is largely by the generous use of porches and verandas, often surrounding the house on two or three sides, together with this floor plan and the free use of louvered windows and doors that Bahamian architecture influenced the houses of Key West.

Built of New England white pine, some of the original random-width, beveled clapboards remain, as well as one wall of flat boards, more common at the time. The porch pillars are square. The most unusual aspect of this and the Roberts house is the low ceilings, common in the Bahamas, but not in Key West. Another interesting feature is the two parallel roofs. This is usually done for the trough effect to catch rain water in the cistern. In all, it is an elegantly designed house in the tradition of the ship-building carpenters—snug, symmetrical, and compact.

The Bartlum family, including son George and his wife Nollie, lived in the house until the early 1900s, when it was sold to Howard W. Sawyer, whose heirs, the James E. Duanes, lived there until 1962. It was purchased at that time by Mr. and Mrs. Youngblood, who did a significant job of restoration, including moving the stairs inside. For a while the Youngbloods ran the house as a museum, and it has been in other private hands and used as a residence since that time. The house remains in excellent condition throughout and is one of the authentic museum pieces of Key West— perhaps deserving the title of granddaddy of the Key West Bahama Houses. Now almost covered with foliage on one side, it is difficult to appreciate from the outside the simple beauty of its lines and the enormous outside gallery space in this architectural gem.

THE ALFONSO-CARRASCO
HOUSE

1001 Eaton Street

This very popular Key West Classical Revival house was built in 1890 by Benito Alfonso, who sold it in 1906 to Antonio Diaz y Carrasco, Cuban consul to the United States. These men were both Cuban émigrés who were loyal to the Cuban revolutionary cause and figured importantly in Key West affairs. The land had been included in the original Pardon C. Greene quarter of John Whitehead's property. It was subsequently purchased in 1875 by James P. Curry, who then sold it to John Lowe, Jr. (As you can

see, a few prominent Key West names seemed to be involved in practically every real estate transaction in town.)

As recently as the 1930s this house was no more than 100 feet from the water's edge. One story has it that Archie Thompson, a rather infamous rum-runner of the day, owned the place and built a second house in the rear to house storage tanks for hiding the rum being unloaded at the nearby docks. The house was later owned by Sloppy Joe Russell, Hemingway's buddy, who started the famous saloon downtown. It was then bought by Senator Bill Neblett and his wife Doris, who lived there until 1977. The house has subsequently been subdivided into several apartments together with the adjoining house in the rear, and is now owned by Cindy and Gary Blum, proprietors of the well-known Cavanaugh's shop on Front Street.

The stately, two-story, rectangular, temple-style Classical Revival structure built shortly after 1890 was in contrast to its neighbors, mostly rather modest frame vernacular and shotgun houses. Originally there was a porch and gallery facing Eaton Street with sculptured wood posts and decorative scroll-cut gingerbread. In about 1912 the porches were continued around the corner, forming a very unusual open Queen Anne style tower, and then all the way down the side to form large verandas, upstairs and down. Legend has it that the upper level of the tower was used for speechmaking to crowds gathered below during political events involving Cuba, such as the 1964 missile crisis.

The stained-glass panel in the front door is of a type seen in a number of Key West houses. The friezes vary from plain square-cut millwork downstairs to the very decorative one upstairs. The brackets look homemade. It is another example of a house which has borrowed features from a number of styles, adapted for Key West, ending up, after modifications, additions, and decorations, as a one-of-a-kind tropical charmer.

THE GINGERBREAD HOUSE
615 Elizabeth Street

Deriving its local name from the elaborate decorations all over its facade, this enormous Conch house is probably the most decorated house in Key West. It was built in 1870 by Benjamin B. Baker and given as a wedding present to his daughter in 1885 when she became Mrs. Illingsworth. It is sometimes referred to as the Baker-Illingsworth House. Of Bahaman origin, Mr. Baker was known as a successful merchant and involved in a number of local enterprises. He served as city commissioner and was actively involved in the sponging and wrecking industries as well as running a furniture store and an undertaking parlor.

The house remained in the Illingsworth family until 1972, when Mrs. Hayden Illingsworth sold it. It has been owned by several parties since that time, most notably Ruth and Charles Munder, who undertook an extensive restoration. All the interior woodwork of heart-of-pine was exposed and is a striking decorative feature of the house. In 1972, when a tornado struck in the area, the house was picked up and blown several feet off its foundation without causing any appreciable damage to the house itself. It was replaced neatly where it remains as one of the most popular architectural attractions in town.

This house is another example of a typical Classical Revival mansion that has been decorated with elaborate Victorian-style gingerbread and then referred to as a Victorian house. The design of the house itself is not characteristic of Victorian era houses at all, as it is quite symmetrical and has none of the features associated with the Victorian style—such as towers, bays, texture variations, verge boards, balconies, little porches, and the like. However, it is generously decorated with very unusual and intricate lacelike millwork in the balustrades and friezes, as well as conspicuous brackets everywhere possible. The under-eaves brackets are Italianate, and the Palladian windows in the pediment are Queen Anne. This house fits the definition of Folk Victorian.

Little else is known about the house other than that it has had numerous owner-occupants and has increased in value astronomically as have many of these captivating and desirable mansions in such a good state of structural and cosmetic restoration.

THE ARTIST HOUSE
534 Eaton Street

Also known as the Otto House, this decorated example of the Queen Anne style was built in 1887 by Thomas Otto, son of the Key West physician, Joseph Otto, after the great fire of 1886 swept the island. Thomas Otto also became a Key West surgeon and lived in this striking house for about forty years. Upon his death the house passed to his son, Eugene Otto.

Gene Otto was a well-known Florida artist and had been living in France where he met his wife, Anne, a concert pianist. They returned to Key West so he could continue his art career. Anne had played piano professionally in the famous Rainbow Room in Radio City, and when she arrived in Key West and began playing at the La Concha Hotel on Duval Street, the room was renamed The Rainbow Room in her honor. The couple were known both for making the house into a richly decorated showplace with elaborate gardens as well as for their lavish entertaining. The Ottos maintained their flamboyant lifestyle in the house for many years until Gene Otto's death in 1974. Their style was continued in the unusual and striking Otto family plot in the Key West Cemetery.

This typically vertical Queen Anne residence is characterized by an octagonal turret rising above two stories of bay windows as well as outdoor staircases connecting the extensive verandas. Decorated with jig-sawn corner brackets, graciously turned pillars, and a multitude of very thin and delicate balusters, the two-story verandas start at the bay windows and extend around to the rear of the house. The overall effect is a striking pattern of angles and shapes.

The ceilings are 12 feet high in the 15 spacious and elaborately decorated rooms. Most of the house is made of virgin yellow pine. It has been described as West Indies Colonial Victorian, a combination not unusual in Key West. The interior is resplendent with its original and very fancy William Morris wallpapers. The house is now operated as a guest house named the Artist House, presumably after Gene Otto and has been painted shades of lavender. According to the present owner, the house was painted successively over the decades of the Ottos' occupancy in pale green, brown, and gold. Although it is somewhat conservative for a Queen Anne house, it is one of the few good examples of this architectural style in Key West.

THE BALDWIN HOUSE
363 Duval Street

Also referred to as the first Key West schoolhouse, this house was built about the same time as the nearby Watlington House, which is referred to as the oldest house in Key West. It was reputed to have been built by, but never occupied by, Alexander Patterson, a very early and quite prominent citizen in Key West, who was active in local affairs and served as mayor at one time. Various sources indicate that the house was occupied by a Mr. and Mrs. Pinckney, whose sister, a Mrs. Passalogue, conducted classes until 1860 and therefore is credited with establishing the first local school. There were a number of private schools in those early days of Key West, opening and closing periodically, as the public school system was not organized and operative until the 1870s. The Pinckneys left in 1852 and the house was bought by John. P. Baldwin, reputed to be a member of an aristocratic British family, though this is not documented. In any case, the Baldwins moved to the Bahamas during the Civil War and returned at war's end to occupy the premises again, and remained for the next several decades. A niece, Miss Annie Baldwin, was the last Baldwin resident of the house.

The house was then purchased in 1962 and completely restored by its present owner and occupant, Edward Knight, who has been active in the restoration movement in Key West. The house presently serves as the offices of the Knight Realty. Restoration included rebuilding the older original house, which served as the dining room and pantry and which had been badly damaged by fire in the 1960s.

This is another imposing Classical Revival house with a Bahamian influence, the latter in the high ceilings, front-to-back wide central hallways, tall shuttered windows, and two-story galleries. The plain window treatment with double-hung sashes, six panes per sash, is reminiscent of the early American Adam style, which continued in the Greek and Classical Revival designs. This gives it the New England look. The original building apparently was a small one and one-half story house and when the newer two-story building was erected, the porch of the older house was removed and attached to the new one by a common wall.

THE RICHARD PEACON HOUSE
712 Eaton Street

This unusual house was built in 1885 by Richard Peacon, the owner of first supermarket in Key West, which was located at 800 Fleming Street. The Peacons moved to Key West from the Bahamas and built their first house on Peacon Lane, which begins across the street from the present house. The larger house was built to have a view to the water down Peacon Lane. Not much is known about the house except that it was occupied by Peacon's daughter, Clara (Mrs. Chester Curry), until it was purchased in 1974 by Angelo Donghia, a nationally known interior decorator. Mr. Donghia had it totally restored and renovated in 1975 by Fred Cole, who made it into one of the showplaces of Key West.

It was purchased in the early 1980s by Calvin Klein, the designer, for the incredible sum of $975,000. This sale made the local papers in large headlines that asked the question, When will houses in Key West pass the $1,000,000 mark? Real estate values, especially of the restored historic houses, had sky-rocketed over a period of a very few years due to the increasing popularity of the island.

The house is a striking variation of the octagonal style of architecture, good examples of which are not to be found in great abundance anywhere. In this instance, the house has an octagonal projection in front of a rather plain square rear section. There is an unusual octagonal pointed cap on the rather flat roof, and two very high-pitched small eaves at either side of the rear section, of no real decorative value and hardly visible from the street. This arrangement suggests that the octagonal projection was a later addition to the building. Inasmuch as it is not a completely octagonal house, this arrangement is often referred to as a "bow front" house. In any case, it is a very impressive, one-of-a-kind Key Wester of great éclat.

THE PATTERSON HOUSE
522 Caroline Street

The original house on this site was that of Col. Alexander Patterson and is pictured in Whitehead's 1838 pencil sketch. The house was destroyed by the fire of 1886. The present house was built before 1889 by George Bowne Patterson, Col. Patterson's son, and remained in the family until the death of his daughter, Etta Patterson in the 1960s. Alexander Patterson was an auctioneer and kept a store at the foot of Whitehead Street. He was a member of the state legislature and was in charge of the naval station at one time. He also served as mayor of Key West.

George B. Patterson held several local and state government posts. He was judge of the sixth district circuit court, United States district attorney for the southern Florida district, and postmaster in Key West. He and his wife, Ida E. Bethel, who was born in the Bahamas, daughter of Judge Winer Bethel, raised six children in this rambling home.

The house was purchased in the 1960s by John M. Spottswood and remains in the Spottswood family. It is occupied by sixth- and seventh-generation Conchs of the Maloney-Bartlum-Spottswood family line.

The Patterson house is an example of Queen Anne style architecture in Key West, although it isn't typically vertical in shape, and might even be better classed as frame vernacular with Queen Anne features and detailing. As with other Key West Queen Annes, it doesn't have all the usual features but is reminiscent of the style in general. The numerous galleries with unusual arched spindlework friezes are distinctive and characteristic of Queen Anne houses. (This kind of detailing is called Eastlake, after Charles Eastlake, an English furniture designer who popularized highly ornamental designs in house decorations.) Porch pillars are turned, and there is a typical Queen Anne, purely decorative, incised, non-balcony with turned pillar at the corner of the second floor. Siding is both shingle and clapboard. Elsewhere this house might have been painted in two or more bright colors. In Key West, however, most houses traditionally were painted white with dark green or black shutters, as in this example.

THE HEMINGWAY HOUSE
907 Whitehead Street

Also known as the Asa Tift house, this most popular tourist attraction now contains the Hemingway Museum. It was originally built in the 1870s in the French Colonial style by Asa Tift, a prominent Key West citizen involved in many business as well as cultural and civic ventures. The house was given to Ernest Hemingway and his second wife, Pauline, in 1931 by her uncle, Gus Pfeiffer. He paid only $8,000 for the house; it was in quite bad condition and needed restoration. Also, it was during the depths of the Depression and the house was in foreclosure.

The Hemingways raised their two sons, Patrick and Gregory, in the house. In 1938, while Hemingway was in Spain covering the Civil War, Pauline had built an olympic-size pool, which was fed by two underground salt-water wells. It was the first private swimming pool in Key West. Hemingway lived and worked in the house until the late 1940s when he and Pauline divorced. She remained in residence until her death in 1951. Although the author no longer occupied the house, he owned it until he sold it in 1961. The present owner, Bernice Dickson, opened the house as a museum in 1964 and it continues to be a heavily attended Key West cultural asset.

The house was made of native limestone blocks excavated from one of the only full basements on the island. Later covered with stucco and remodeled, it shows elements of several architectural styles. The basic house is a square box with flat roof. This house is described elsewhere as built originally in the Spanish Colonial style. However, there are no evidences of this style anywhere in this building. The extensive cast-iron pillars, verandas, and balusters are in the French Colonial style, introduced and popular in the Vieux Carré in New Orleans in the mid-1800s, and were brought from New Orleans by ship by Mr. Tift. The full-length two-paned glazed arched windows are Italianate, appearing for the first time in American houses mid-nineteenth century. The Second Empire mansard roof noted elsewhere in descriptions of this house is not on the main house. It was added to a former carriage house to make Hemingway's studio on the second floor, which was connected to the main house by a catwalk. The mansard roof is one of two in Key West. (See description of the J.Y. Porter House.) The house is the only one of its kind in Key West.

BIBLIOGRAPHY

Barber, Claudia I. and John Viele. *John Bartlum: Key West's Premier Shipbuilder*. The Florida Keys Sea Heritage Journal, Volume 1, No. 3 (Spring, 1991).

Browne, Jefferson H. *Key West: The Old and the New*. Facsimile reproduction of 1912 edition Gainesville, Florida: University of Florida Press, 1973.

Cox, Christopher. *Key West Companion*. New York: St Martin's Press, 1983.

Davidson, William H. *Pine Log and Greek Revival*. Chattahoochie Valley Historical Society. Alexander City, Alabama: Outlook Publishing Company, 1964.

Early, James. *Romanticism and American Architecture*. New York: A.S. Barnes, 1965.

Gamble, Robert. *Historic Architecture in Alabama: A Primer of Styles and Types, 1810-1930*. Tuscaloosa, Alabama: University of Alabama Press, 1990.

Jakle, John A., Robert W. Bastian and Douglas K. Meyer. *Common Houses in American Small Towns*. Athens: University of Georgia Press, 1989.

Lancaster, Clay. *The American Bungalow*. New York: Abbeville Press, 1985.

Little, Jr., Edward J. "The Historical Role of Fisheries of the Florida Keys during the Nineteenth Century." *The Florida Keys Sea Heritage Journal*, Vol. 1, No 2. (Winter, 1990).

McAlester, Virginia and Lee. *A Field Guide to American Houses*. New York: Alfred A. Knopf, 1990.

McArdle, A. deC and D.B. *Carpenter Gothic*. New York: Watson-Guptill Publications, 1978.

McLendon, James. *Papa: Hemingway in Key West*. Key West, Florida: Langley Press, Inc., 1972 (revised 1990). Schuler, Stanley. *Mississippi Valley Architecture*. Exton, Pennsylvania: Schiffer, 1984.

Starr, Roger. "The Carpenter-Architects of Key West." *American Heritage Magazine*, Volume 23, No. 2 (February, 1975) .

Toledano, Roulhac B. and Mary Louise Christovich. *New Orleans Architecture Series, Vol. VI, Faubourg Treme and the Bayou Road*. New Orleans: Pelican Publishing Company, 1989.

Toledano, Roulhac B., et al. *New Orleans Architecture Series, Vol. IV, The Creole Faubourgs*. New Orleans: Pelican Publishing Company, 1989.

Vlach, John Michael. *Sources of the Shotgun House: African and Caribbean Antecedents for Afro-American Architecture*. Ph.D. Thesis, Indiana University, 1975.

Wells, Sharon and Lawson Little. *Portraits: Wooden Houses of Key West*. Key West, Florida: Historic Key West Preservation Board, 1982.

The following have no author listed:

Cultural Resource Survey of Key West #48. Key West, Florida: Bureau of Historic Sites and Properties, Division of Archives, History and Records Management, Miscellaneous Project Report Series, 1976.

The New and Greater Key West Florida: Told in Picture and Story. 1990 facsimile of 1914 edition, published by J.A. Willis under the auspices of the Key West Board of Trade.

Palliser's American Architecture, or Everyman a Complete Builder. 1888.

Preservation Guidebook for the Section of the City of Key West. Old Island Restoration Commission, 1975.

GLOSSARY

architrave — lower molding of entablature directly above capital of column.

baluster — individual support of balustrade.

balustrade — exterior partial wall consisting of railings and balusters or other decorative pieces, usually on porches, decks, or roof edges.

board and batten — vertical sheathing with strips covering joints between boards.

capital — decorative item at top of column.

chamfered — beveled.

cornice — upper molding of entablature above frieze.

dentils — small blocks of wood attached evenly to moldings, usually the cornice, for decoration.

entablature — series of moldings above classical order of columns – including cornice, frieze, and architrave.

frieze — middle molding of entablature.

gallery — incised porch on second story.

glazed panel —glass pane.

incised porch — porch cut under main roof of house.

quatrefoils — decorative items in Gothic Revival style, usually in place of capitals.

hip roof — roof without eaves; rectangular pyramidal roof.

lights, window and door — individual glass panels of window or door.

mansard roof — roof in which near-vertical roof part forms wall of top story, with flat roof over most of story.

millwork — manufactured decorative wood parts creating intricate designs.

mortise-and-tendon joint — joint fixed by cutting parts to fit into each other.

pediment — triangular area under eaves of temple style house.

piers — corner blocks of wood or stone upon which frame of house rests.

pillars — porch supports, similar to columns.

portico — entry porch with columns extending from facade of house.

roof-plate — upper beam of top story wall supporting roof members.

scuttle — opening or "hatch" in roof with removable lid for light and ventilation.

sill — base beam of frame resting on foundation or piers.

soffit board — ceiling piece under over-hang of roof.

spandrels — triangular area between arch and moldings of porch bays.

spindlework — lathe-turned decorative pieces, usually part of frieze.

surround, window or door — framing elements around windows and doors.

veranda — porch extending to a second side of house.

vergeboards — decorative board under eaves.

If you enjoyed reading this book, here are some other Pineapple Press titles you might enjoy as well. To request our complete catalog or to place an order, write to Pineapple Press, P.O. Box 3889, Sarasota, Florida 34230, or call 1-800-PINEAPL (746-3275). Or visit our website at www.pineapplepress.com.

Over Key West and the Florida Keys by Charles Feil. Full-color aerial shots of shimmering ocean, uninhabited mangrove islands, bridges and causeways, vintage neighborhoods, and million-dollar homes. An appealing blend of descriptive text and dreamy images that capture the beauty and uniqueness of the Florida Keys. A beautiful coffee-table book. ISBN 1-56164-240-1 (hb)

Key West Gardens and Their Stories by Janis Frawley-Holler. Venture off the beaten track and enjoy beautiful views of the islanders' sanctuaries as well as fascinating stories and histories of the grounds where gardens now grow. Full color throughout. ISBN 1-56164-204-5 (pb)

Florida Keys Impressions by Millard Wells. Famed watercolorist Millard Wells offers his unique impressions of the Keys, with their blend of Caribbean cultures, interesting architecture, lush vegetation, laid-back attitude, and beautiful tropical marine environment. ISBN 1-56164-209-6 (hb)

Hemingway's Key West Second Edition by Stuart McIver. A rousing, true-to-life portrait of Hemingway in Key West, Cuba, and Bimini during his heyday. Includes a two-hour walking tour of the author's favorite Key West haunts and a narrative of the places he frequented in Cuba. ISBN 1-56164-241-X (pb)

Classic Cracker by Ronald W. Haase. A study of Florida's wood-frame vernacular architecture that traces the historical development of the regional building style, including single-pens, double-pens, dog trots, and shotgun houses. ISBN 1-56164-014-X (pb)

The Houses of St. Augustine by David Nolan. A history of the city told through its buildings, from the earliest coquina structures, through Colonial and Victorian times, to the modern era. Color photographs and original watercolors. ISBN 1-56164-0697 (hb); ISBN 1-56164-075-1 (pb)

Historic Homes of Florida by Laura Stewart and Susanne Hupp. Seventy-four notable dwellings throughout the state—all open to the public—tell the human side of history. Each home is illustrated by H. Patrick Reed or Nan E. Wilson. ISBN 1-56164-085-9 (pb)

Historical Traveler's Guide to Florida by Eliot Kleinberg. Visit Henry Plant's Tampa hotel, the wreck of the *San Pedro,* and Ernest Hemingway's Key West home. Here are 57 travel destinations in Florida of historical significance. ISBN 1-56164-122-7 (pb)

Florida's Finest Inns and Bed & Breakfasts by Bruce Hunt. From warm and cozy bed & breakfasts to elegant and historic hotels, this is the definitive guide to Florida's most quaint, romantic, and often eclectic lodgings. With photos and charming pen-and-ink drawings by the author. ISBN 1-56164-202-9 (pb)

Florida's Museums and Cultural Attractions by Doris Bardon and Murray Laurie. A great take-along guide to over 350 sites around the state. Also takes you to historic neighborhoods, cafes, shops, and art galleries within walking distance of each site. ISBN 1-56164-162-6 (pb)